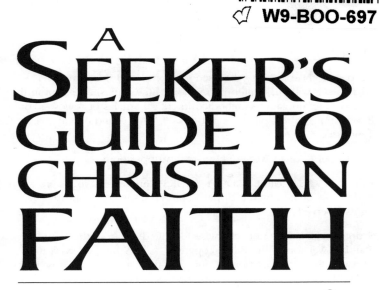

A SEEKER'S GUIDE TO CHRISTIAN FAITH

FROM UPPER ROOM MINISTRIES®

BEN CAMPBELL JOHNSON

UPPER
ROOM BOOKS™
NASHVILLE

Cover design: Gore Studio, Inc.
Cover art: "Resurrection" © 1996 by Anne C. Brink
Interior design: Jonathan C. Setzer
First printing: 2000

Library of Congress Cataloging-in-Publication Data

Johnson, Ben Campbell.
  A seeker's guide to Christian faith / Ben Campbell Johnson/
    p. cm.
  ISBN 0-8358-0907-2
  1. Christian life. I. Title.

BV4501.2 J53854 2000
230—dc21   99-462259
                                                        CIP

Printed in the United States of America

Before we begin...

I'd like for you to know a bit about me. You should know that I began life outside any organized religion, not as a pagan, just ignorant. My parents were good people but not religious until my later years. We were relatively poor, rural, and limited in education. With no faith to shield me against the terrors of my childhood imagination, I feared the monsters that lurked in the darkness surrounding me. Feelings of inadequacy and inferiority also filled me.

When I was nine years old we moved to town, a mere village of fifteen hundred people. It was in this county-seat town that I had an encounter with God, a subject that has fascinated me for over five decades. In all these years I've been getting acquainted with the great mystery of faith, and have spent countless hours gathering with God's people, trying to learn the Christian language, and delighting in the surprises of Christian fellowship. I've never been a star believer, more a meat and potatoes person slugging it out in the trenches of life, learning to doubt my doubts and marvel at the divine mystery of being.

As I look back over the years that I've been on this journey, I think that I know some things about God. If you have an interest in getting acquainted with a God who knows all about you already, I think I can be of help. I have spent over twenty-five years in school and have earned five degrees, but what qualifies me to walk beside you on your journey is that I know God.

In each of the adventures recounted in this book I will write to you like a friend in a nearby city. I'll talk with you about one of the tiny things that's important in knowing God and living the godly life. Then I'll offer you a little experiment to practice. As you let these ideas sink in and as you take God more seriously, amazing things will begin to happen in your life. I suspect you will begin to discover meaning in your life in ways you have never known before. Over time, the evidence will begin to multiply that you are transacting with infinite wisdom and goodness!

As we begin this journey together, I am asking you to trust me to be a friend. I have told you about part of my own life so that we can begin with a basis for trust. As we explore different aspects of a life with God, you will have many opportunities to evaluate my guidance. I have no private agenda for your life. I will clearly and simply describe different aspects of life before God, illustrate the principle or experience with stories or metaphors, and then I will offer you a simple way to begin practicing the faith. This relationship between us takes on peculiar meaning when you consider we are dealing with the most important thing in the universe.

Ben Johnson

1 FIRST GUIDANCE: *Sensing a Direction for Your Life*

Simple things mark our lives and distinguish one day from another. Things like birthdays, visits with friends, meeting someone you love when you return home from work, or sharing a meal with someone important to you. Memories of these events fill us with delight. Other marker events also appear in our lives, markers that remind us of loss, misdirection, and failure. Sometimes it doesn't feel good to recall these turning points. These marker events are, nonetheless, part of our lives, part of the force that shapes who we are today and possibly where we will be tomorrow.

I have found it helpful to look at the turning points in my life as a way of getting my bearing. Sometimes we treat our lives like a ball of clay; we resist patting, forming, and opening it up because we fear that some long-buried memory will arise to threaten us. Those who continue to resist examining their lives become like clay baked in the oven—hard, fixed, and impenetrable. By contrast, when you actually take a look at your life, you discover the monster that you feared so deeply seldom rears its head. But you do discover trends, gain insights into connections with things past, find meaning in simple things you never noticed, and gather clues about the meaning of your life. Because such reflections on my life have been so very important, I'd like to show you a way to look at your life and listen to what it is saying.

On a sheet of paper, or the back of an envelope, draw a line from top to bottom. At the bottom of the line write "I was born" and at the top of the line write "Now." Begin with your birth or as far back as you can remember and move forward noting the turning points in your life. At each turning point make a hash mark on the vertical line and write a couple of words that denote the event that caused the change in your life.

A turning point is an event, person, or insight that changes the texture of your life. For example, your life was much the same until you moved to a new town or neighborhood. The move created a turning point. Life from that point forward changed for you—new friends, different activities, and fresh opportunities. Move through your life, jotting down all the turning points from your earliest memory all the way to the present. Be sure to make a hash mark on your vertical line and name the turning point.

When you finish making the list, read over the turning points slowly. Now close your eyes and picture the movement of your life from turning point to turning point, until you come to "Now!" Review your life one more time from the top down, from "Now" to your birth. This time move more quickly through the list of turning points.

Then pause. Be still. Listen to your life! What is your life about? Does it seem to you that something inside you is trying to express itself?

In all likelihood, you passed over pain in some of the turning points. Don't be afraid of your pain. Acknowledge it and let it be. Later on we will deal with it but for now simply acknowledge it and move on. Just know that most of us have shame or pain tucked away in the corner of our souls. Remember, don't run from your pain.

Now think of the spaces on your vertical line between the turning points or markers as chapters of your life. If you were writing an autobiography what would you name each of these chapters? Take time to think about what was going on in your life at that time. Who were the important people? What were the life-shaping experiences? Spend fifteen minutes thinking about your life, its movement, pain, distractions, and discoveries. Out of these memories, name the chapters. The titles of your chapters should reflect the tone of what was occurring in your life during the period.

After you have thought about these things, notice how you feel. Be still and let the feeling of being here now soak in. There is more for us to do with this lifeline. But for now be content with simply feeling the flow of your life as if it were a stream flowing through time and space bringing you to this moment.

2 SECOND GUIDANCE: *Wondering About the Mysteries*

"**Y**ou are a unique, unrepeatable miracle of God!" The consultant who was giving guidance to the organization I directed spoke these exact words to me. The words echoed in my mind for months and became something like a mantra. "Unique"—not another person in the world exactly like me. "Unrepeatable"—there never will be another person just like me. "Miracle of God"—an expression of the creative power of the one who made the world. How amazing it is to be a human being in this wonderful world!

One day while I was conducting a session with a group of church leaders from different parts of the country, a woman, whom I will call Anna, made a bold and revealing statement. Anna said, "I think I may have had experiences of God but I do not know how to put them into words. There have been times when I have known which path to take but I cannot tell how I knew." Here was a person who had distant memories of faint brushes with the spirit of God. Somehow the touch with the divine had never crystallized in her thinking with sufficient clarity to speak of it. Perhaps she did not have words to name and grasp the meaning of her experience. I suggested that a worthy project for her during the ten-day gathering would be to reflect on her ordinary experiences in life to see if she noted evidence of God's activity.

I wonder if there might be something in this woman's story that sounds like your own. When you think about your life, have inexplicable things happened to you? Have there been moments when it seemed as though a presence surrounded or held you? Do you recall significant persons coming into your life at a particular time for no special reason? All these experiences point to what I like to call "brushes with the mystery."

In recent years I have become convinced that wondering about these kinds of experiences is often a prelude to a genuine faith in God. Wonder serves as a key to unlock the meaning of these "brushes with the mystery."

Wonder is both a noun and a verb. Wonder (noun) cannot be induced, controlled, or dismissed at will. For example, have you ever been thinking about a particular person, and when the phone rings, it is that very person calling you? An occurrence like this evokes wonder. Or, have you ever seen a sunset that explodes in your imagination with a sense of beauty and something within you shouts, "Wow!" Wonder has a way of shaking up your customary ways of seeing and believing. Sometimes it produces a kind of ecstasy that drives you out of yourself.

Wonder as a verb is somewhat different from wonder as a noun. You can initiate, direct, and expand your wonder about things, persons, and events. The verb "to wonder" is a walking-around word that enables you to muse over things, question them, and inquire of their significance.

Our lives are filled with happenings that provoke our wondering why. We wonder why a person comes into our life at a particular time. Or, we wonder at the sequence of events that bring joy and fulfillment to our lives. From one point of view, the events were merely chance things, but upon closer investigation some purpose seems to have been woven into the fabric of the occurrences. As Christian communicator Frederick Buechner has remarked, "The question is not whether the things that happen to you are chance things or God's things because, of course, they are both at once."

After the general meeting, I asked Anna, the woman to whom I referred earlier, to talk with me. In the course of our conversation I invited her to create a vertical lifeline from birth to now, just as I asked you to do in the previous guidance. I then invited her to think deeply about each of the turns in her life, each of the significant persons, and the times of joy and the painful times of failure. "And," I said, "as you think about these events, wonder where God may have been in them. Wonder what God might have been doing in your life through those events." A few days later Anna came to my office and exclaimed how utterly amazed she was at what had happened to her. She had seen the hand of mystery open to her. She had a glimpse of the reality of God being in her ordinary life. The unnamed mystery was getting a face and a character. This is my hope for you as you begin to wonder about your life.

Perhaps it will help if I review several turning points in my life. My first marker is "Move to Town." This simple event may appear inconsequential to an outsider. What possible significance could moving a mere six miles have for a child's life? When I pause to wonder, the meaning becomes obvious to me.

Before moving to town, I never attended church. I knew nothing about God and the name Jesus Christ was strange to me. Already by nine years of age I had experienced the terrors of childhood without a protective covering of faith.

Once we moved and got settled in this new community, my mother took me to the church. I remember the teacher telling me about Jesus and teaching me songs of the faith. Although I did not understand the meaning of the words "Jesus loves me this I know," these very words would one day change my life.

So when I review the first turning point in my life, I clearly recognize how it is filled with implications for the years that followed. Do you see how wonder begins to open up the meaning of events in our lives? This kind of wonder is also the prelude to knowledge and it is the anteroom of faith.

I have spent time describing wonder and relating my own experience of wondering to you because I'm sure you also have felt the power of amazement in your life. You've been struck with wonder and have experienced the act of wondering. But I want to help you look at your life again through the lenses of wonder. Pull out that lifeline you created and notice the turning point.

I invite you to look at the movement of your life and begin to wonder where God has been hidden in the events of your life. Take one turning point, for example, and begin to think about it. Note the setting of your life at the time. Put all the characters in place. Recall what was happening then in your world. Now, wonder where God was in this chapter of your life. Or, if you can't quite claim a definite presence, where might God have been? What was God seeking to do in this period of your life? Don't answer too quickly. Wonder and listen to the intuitions that come to you. Sometimes insights come in astounding ways when you least expect them.

THIRD GUIDANCE: *Imagining a New Beginning*

I have heard people say, "I cannot imagine what it would be like to have a relationship with God." When people begin to think about God in relation to themselves, the screen of their mind is either blank or fuzzy. They have made a true and honest confession. They cannot imagine God as part of their life in any positive, transformative way.

I suspect that when people make this statement they generally have negative images of God and themselves, if they have images at all. The notion of God being close to them causes anxiety or shame or guilt, and they feel repulsed by the thought of God. Or the thought of God has no relevance to them at all and they ignore it. To begin the imaginative process, you might muse over these questions:

- What would it be like for a person to have a personal experience of the Creator God?
- What would it feel like?
- What difference would it make?
- How do you begin even to imagine a human relation to the infinite God?

I've wondered about the best way to help with these questions about the human experience of God. I do not have an exhaustive answer, nor do I have a final answer. But I do have a personal answer. My musing over these searching questions brought back the memory of my own awakening to God and it occurred to me that my story might provide a model to help you think about your relationship. Again, I repeat the warning that my story is not a model for you to follow but one that can help you think about your own story.

My life in relation to God began as a blank page. I often think it was white with splotches of black here and there. The white part symbolized being loved by my parents—in particular, a close relationship with my mother—and the delight of an extended family. The black patches spoke of my deep childhood fears, the terror I felt about the monsters when they stuck up their heads out of my unconsciousness.

I never went to church or heard anyone speak of God until I was about nine years old. The whole religious world was unknown to me. At the edges of my consciousness there seemed to be a dark, mysterious world that loomed beyond me. As a child of nine or ten, it dawned upon me that one day I would die. The thought of my death terrified me so deeply that I often found it hard to go to sleep for fear I wouldn't wake up. These images, fears, and anxieties often came to me during the early years of my life when I knew nothing of God's sheltering love.

One of the sources of wonderment in my life occurred about the time my family moved from a rural community into town. This new setting made it easy for my mother to take me to church. She enrolled me in Sunday school where I learned words like *God, Jesus, Bible,* and *love.* Perhaps one of the most important gifts of this preparation period was the knowledge of Christian role models. People appeared in my life, often the parents of my friends, who read the Bible, prayed, and spoke about God as if God were present and real. I'd never met people like this before.

There were also a few experiences at church functions that seemed to shape my understanding of God. One day in the school cafeteria an amazing thing happened. A classmate asked this question: "If Jesus were here today, would you be on his side?"

My answer was quick and simple. "No."

Recounting these early experiences makes me wonder how it all came about. Why did it happen like it did?

The answer to the question about "being on Jesus' side" led to an invitation to attend special meetings being conducted at our church. My classmate thought they would interest me. I don't know if interest is the right word for the experience, but attending the sessions made a strong impact on my life. I listened to the speaker. He invited us to yield to the spirit of Jesus. I desired to open my life to God's spirit. At the time I did not know how to ask God for anything or even explain to God what it was that I was seeking. What was so utterly amazing was the fact that God knew me deeper than any words I could have said. God met me without doubt in a manner that I cannot explain. In a gentle, loving, and very real way, God became known to me.

The beginning of this fragile but significant connection with God seemed to have immediate effects on my life. I felt loved and valued by the creator of the universe. God knew me and cared about me. I felt at peace with myself, something I had never known before. The darkness and fear that pervaded my consciousness was dispelled by light. I had a budding assurance of who I was and my life seemed to have a purpose.

The one outstanding memory I have of those early days of my relationship with God was the deep urge I felt to tell everyone I knew about the mystery of a relationship with God. I told different people in my life how God had become real to me. And I asked them to tell me what they knew about this God who had become personal to me. Along with the passion to talk about this new reality I felt a desire to talk with God. I began as a novice learning something about what Christians call prayer. I had never opened a Bible before. My compelling interest in the Bible got me reading the various little books and letters and that's when I discovered that I needed glasses. I had never been as intent in my studies as I had become in reading the scriptures.

Going to church on Sunday was also a very different experience. One of my clearest memories from the early days of going to church centers on the offering. I worked at a bus station café before and after school. I think I was paid about $20 per week. The first week after I met God, I pulled two dollar bills from my pocket and placed them in the offering plate. My mentors had taught me that God's people give a tithe, ten percent of their earnings. I cannot describe how proud I felt to have a part in God's work.

This is a simple story. But I offer it to you as one example of how God got my attention, loved me, and then drew me into a significant relationship. One thing I am sure of, your experience will be different from mine and this is as it should be. The details of how God comes to us are not important; it is the fact of a relationship that is important.

To begin constructing your relationship from darkness to light, from unknowing to believing, or from idols to God, review your lifeline. I have already invited you to wonder about why things happened as they did, why certain persons came into your life, and where God might have been. I think it will now benefit you to return to that lifeline, meditate on the different shifts in your life, and begin to put together your own account of getting to know God. You will be in for a happy discovery.

FOURTH GUIDANCE: *Building on the Rock*

In the Bible there is a very interesting and important conversation between Jesus and Simon Peter, one of the disciples. Jesus asked his followers, "Who do you say that I am?"

> Simon Peter answered, "You are the Messiah, the Son of the living God." And Jesus answered him, "Blessed are you, Simon son of Jonah! For flesh and blood has not revealed this to you, but my Father in heaven. And I tell you, you are Peter, and on this rock I will build my church, and the gates of Hades will not prevail against it." (Matthew 16:16-18)

This conversation between Jesus and Peter holds great significance for the Christian faith because it is the first time that one of Jesus' followers recognized his true identity. It is not my purpose to explore the depth of meaning in this dialogue but to point to one emphasis, Jesus' description of Peter as a rock.

Peter, whose name means "rock," answered Jesus' question about his identity with these words, "You are the Son of the living God." What an amazing insight for Peter! Jesus recognized it with an affirmation. "Flesh and blood [a human being] has not revealed this to you, but my Father in heaven." God showed Peter who Jesus was and he confessed it aloud for all to hear.

"Upon this rock," Jesus said, "I will build my church." When Jesus asked "Whom do you say that I am," Peter replied, "You are the Christ, the Son of the living God." The rock upon which Jesus built was neither Peter nor his confession. Jesus constructed the church upon himself, on his own person. Jesus is the rock upon which the church rests. The rock upon which Jesus builds is not, then, the confession itself but the one whom Peter confessed, Jesus himself. In brief, whoever builds upon Jesus Christ builds upon the rock.

In another place in the Bible, Jesus tells a story about two persons who build houses: one person builds a house upon a rock and the other builds on sand. When the storms came, the house built on sand collapsed but the one built on rock endured (Matt. 7:24-27). Obviously, Jesus did not mean this story to be a lesson in carpentry or architecture. He was speaking about what we base our lives on. When we put Peter's confession alongside Jesus' story of the two houses, the message seems obvious: wise people base their lives on Christ.

All of us have been given a life, and we must build it on something. Think about your life. What are you building on? What do you count on when the chips are down? What holds you steady when reversals come into your life?

What endures when everything else fails? The answer to these questions for me has been Christ.

I have no intention to lay out a case for building your life on Christ. I could do that but my interest is in offering you a testimony about this rock. To illustrate the sturdiness and dependability of this foundation, I want to tell you about a few times when my life might have collapsed it if had not been for Christ the rock.

Before I came to know him I had no idea who I was or what I was to do with my life. In the earliest days of my relationship with him, he gave me a dream for my life, not fully formed but clear enough to follow a step at a time. I saw through his presence that my life could count for something greater than myself. I could help people. I could help to make a different world. I could find meaning for my own life.

A few years after meeting this God I have described to you, I began to experience the old feelings of fear and dark clouds hung over my head. Sometimes I heard accusations in my head. "You are a phony." "You don't believe this stuff." Why don't you give up and quit?" No matter how loud the voices of despair screamed, I found myself upon a rock. He held me when I could not hold myself. Honestly, some days I wondered if I would survive, but he gave me the strength to face myself and the pain of my inner world. I found him to be a rock.

When I was thirty-three my father died. He had cancer and lasted for about six months. His terminal illness brought grief to me but it also forced me to look at my own mortality. Facing my own death honestly caused me to put a lot of weight on the rock. Not too many years later my mother had an early onset of Alzheimer's and she spent fourteen years in a nursing home. A dozen of those years she did not even know who I was. But the rock was firm in the shakiness of my grief.

I have found this rock to be solid when my sense of direction in life has brought risk. In midlife I felt a call to return to school for a graduate degree. When I responded to this call, I had no money, no job, nor did I have a house to move into. With a wife and a child to support, I felt anxious about my providing their basic necessities. In an unexpected move a mentor obtained rent for a house for us to live in. A friend assisted with tuition. God opened opportunities for weekend work that provided money to meet basic needs.

One of my most painful and frightening moments came when I recognized that I was in an unworkable, destructive marriage. After twenty years, ten years of which had been spent in marriage counseling, the relationship got worse and the pain grew more intense. Get a divorce? Everything in me rebelled against the idea. What were my options? I had tried all that I knew to have a good marriage but I failed. Coming to the decision to divorce was the scariest decision I ever made. Stripped of that relationship, I didn't know who I was anymore. People questioned my integrity, even the authenticity of my faith. Life was tough but the rock did not move under the load. I experienced him with me, beside me, and before me, showing the way.

These short vignettes number but a few of the stories of his faithfulness and strength in my life. I hope very much that you will not think that I am bragging or minimizing my own faults or failures. I do not intend to do that. I hope that you see in these tiny pictures of my pain and failures the rock who has been beneath me with an incredible strength. Christ has shown me repeatedly that I don't have to be good or perfect or right to be loved and sustained by God's presence.

In conclusion, I have told you these things with the hope that you may come to believe that Jesus is a rock you can rest your life on, a foundation that the worst experiences in your life will not shake, and a loving presence that will see you through everything.

Think back over your life and name the center that you have depended on to hold life together (parents, money, friends, work, achievement, etc.). Consider what it might be like for you to build your life on the rock. Could this become a desirable choice for you?

5 FIFTH GUIDANCE: *Seeking Answers*

Inside each of us there is a void or a hunger that keeps yearning for answers to the deepest questions of our lives. Strangely, we cannot shut off the questions; they are as natural as breathing. Perhaps you have found yourself asking questions, seeking answers, or trying to resolve your own restlessness for a long time. Have you wondered why you cannot find the solution to the craving?

One of the great Christians who lived hundreds of years ago once said, "O God, you have made us for yourself and our hearts are restless until they rest in you." I think this man, Augustine, was pointing to the same yearning that many of us feel today, a longing to find an answer to the puzzle of our lives.

This yearning and questioning is more widespread than I had originally suspected. My perspective was stretched by a group of sincere and honest persons in New York City. I had been invited to lead a special event at the Marble Collegiate Church on Fifth Avenue, the church led for so many years by Dr. Norman Vincent Peale.

The senior minister who followed Dr. Peale, Arthur Caliandro, and I offered a dialogue to the congregation one Sunday. I spoke in the evening. At the conclusion of the evening's presentation the coordinator of the event said, "Tomorrow evening at 6:00 P.M. we will have a Q&A session with Ben." This announcement sent a chill down my spine.

The anxiety I felt about an evening of questions and answers did not arise because of the hard questions I would be asked; I was frightened because I couldn't believe anyone would give up an evening to engage in dialogue with me. All day Monday I worried about no one coming. I feared the embarrassment of being stood up. They had announced that the meeting would be held in the social hall, a venue that can seat two hundred people. But I imagined that we could hold the gathering in a coat closet. I tormented myself all day with images of rejection, failure, and shame.

Yet the evening yielded something different. When I arrived at the church at about 5:30 for the 6:00 P.M. Q&A session, I was told that the original gathering place had already filled to capacity. A decision had been made to move the session into the church sanctuary. By 6:00 P.M. more than three hundred and fifty people had found a seat.

The format was simple. Every person had been given a three-by-four-inch card upon entering. Each was instructed to write any question on the card and pass it to the aisle. The stack of cards was then handed to me and I responded to the first question and began to work my way through the stack.

As I read one question after another, I offered short, succinct answers like the following:

- If you could sum up in one sentence what it means to be a Christian, what would it be?
  One sentence. To be a Christian is to have a personal relationship with God through Jesus Christ that changes us from antagonists into friends and seekers after God's will.

- Why, when I find a place in life that feels right and balanced and whole, do I blink my eye and there I am, right back at the beginning again?
  No posture or attitudinal or emotional state in life can be frozen. All of us are in a constant state of change whether we like it or not. But we should remember that God rides the changes with us.

- How do I know if I am on the right path in my search?
  The answer, of course, is determined by what you are searching for! I assume that you mean your search for God. When you seek to know more about God, when you talk with folks who know God, and when your life begins to show the influence of Jesus Christ, you are on the right track. Usually people on the way to God show love, humility, and concern for others.

- How do you get closer to God?
  Deepening your relationship with God has many of the characteristics of deepening your relationship with someone you love. Spend time with God. Learn more about God. Talk with God about the deepest feelings and concerns in your life. Don't keep secrets. Let trust develop.

- What am I to do when I feel an emptiness inside and a longing for something but I don't know what?

Ultimately, your longing is for God. Pay attention to your longing. It is like a pigeon's homing instinct. It will lead you to God.

For more than two and one-half hours all these people sat and listened to questions and answers. About midway through the session I invited a few bold persons to come to the platform and ask their questions aloud. A dozen or more lined up waiting their turn. The interchange was challenging, refreshing, and encouraging to me as well as to the participants. When the session ended, I was amazed that so many had come and stayed for so long.

Inspired by this experience in New York City, I held similar sessions in Chicago, Los Angeles, and Atlanta. The same results followed. People were eager to ask questions, to discuss answers, and to gain deeper insight into themselves and the issues of their lives.

I have related this experience to you for two reasons. First, I want you to know that it is okay for you to have questions about God and about how to become related to God. Second, I want you to know that the hunger evidenced by these questions has inspired the content and form of this book. Although I have not written here in a question-and-answer format, the experience I had with young adults in four corners of the nation has shaped my thinking and guided what I have written for you.

Before you proceed, I suggest that you review the First and Second Guidances and seek to find the gnawing question with which you are living today.

6 SIXTH GUIDANCE: Naming Your Hunger

*Wise men from the East came to Jerusalem, asking,
"Where is the child who has been born
king of the Jews? For we observed his star
at its rising, and have come to pay him homage.*

This is a statement made about persons seeking to see
Jesus when he was first born. As you have rummaged
around in your life, you may have uncovered a hunger for
something more. Life has offered you a certain kind of
fullness, but you will feel a hunger for that unnamed thing
that somehow has evaded you. For a very long time,
perhaps, you have felt this yearning for peace and
fulfillment. You are not unlike numerous fellow travelers
who have been driven in their choices by the desire for
something more.

Twenty centuries ago three strange characters—
soothsayers or astrologers, we might say—left Iran to
follow a star. They believed this unusual star would guide
them to the great treasure, the "something more" that they
were seeking. What do you suppose people thought about
this entourage moving through the country in a camel
caravan? Who were these wealthy men bearing gifts of
various sorts? These strange horoscope readers who set out
on a journey from the home country to a strange country
epitomize thousands of persons who today are on their
search for the answer to the deep questions of their lives.

The three astrologers sought to complete their quest by
following a star and it led them to a manger in Bethlehem
where Jesus was born. Some years later another man
seeking a star to follow said to Jesus, "I will follow you

wherever you go." This eager soul desired to be a disciple but he was unaware that Jesus was without a bed to sleep in or the finances to underwrite his followers. He felt an urge toward the new life but had not counted the cost.

Restless spirits can find calm. Confused persons can find direction. And anxious hearts can find peace. It is possible. In volumes of religious literature countless persons give witness to the fact that women and men have found an answer to the human quest for peace and for meaning. The soul with all its yearnings can be fulfilled with something it did not create and someone it does not control. Truly, the answer lies beyond ourselves in one who is greater than us.

In your search for "a star to follow," by which I mean a way of life to pursue, demand of this pattern of life four things. First, choose a way of life that has a long and rich tradition. A strong tradition has stood the test of time by adapting to changing circumstances. Second, choose a faith that makes sense to you. If you have a conflict between a hodgepodge of Eastern religion, a self-centered spiritualism, and a Christian faith that for twenty centuries has challenged the best minds, your choice should be obvious. Third, choose a way of life that others have found meaningful and who give positive testimony to its worth. Finally, don't choose a way of life because it is easy, but choose one that challenges you to be your best.

Some years ago when I was seeking a way to live my life, I asked these questions to help make a decision. I chose the Christian faith. It has a long memory reaching back over twenty centuries to Jesus Christ who lived, died, rose again, and is present with us today. Some of the best minds this world has produced claimed this faith as their own. I think also of the testimony of martyrs who died for their faith as a witness to its truth and value. I call to mind the nuns in El Salvador who died at the hands of lawless rebels and Martin Luther King Jr. who died seeking justice for his race. There are millions of others who live lives of kindness, mercy, and unselfishness making the world a decent place to live. When I think of the depth of their faith it challenges the very best within me. I want to be all that I can be and the Christian way offers me this challenge. Best of all, it offers forgiveness when I fail.

Have you chosen a way of life or have you haphazardly fallen into one? Ask yourself a few revealing questions:

- What is really important to me?
- Where did I get my values?
- On what grounds do I make my decisions?
- What is the goal of my life?

I dare say that your answers to these four soul-searching questions reflect the culture in which you have grown up. With a degree of hesitation, I'm going to risk sketching answers some typical persons might give.

I suspect that you may have said that being happy or successful or having financial independence is important to you. Do you think that your values have mostly come from the media—newspaper, television, and the movies? Perhaps some values have family fingerprints on them.

Are your grounds for decision making centered on yourself? Do you make most of your decisions on the basis of what will please you, benefit you, help you get ahead, or make you look good? Finally, do you think the aim of life is to seek pleasure and fulfillment of your wants?

If my hunches are correct, you have found yourself nodding your head as you read these questions. If these issues matter to you, you need more than a new philosophy or psychological gimmick; you need a religious tradition to help you answer the most basic questions in your life.

You see, we are not the first persons to ponder the issue of who we are, why we are here, and the purpose and direction of our lives. Millions before us have embraced Christian faith as a framework within which to grapple with these issues.

I am not selling Christian faith. It doesn't need selling; it needs testing through experience. I am a Christian and I testify that it has led me to peace, fulfillment, and meaning. Christ has freed me from the fear of death. I would invite you to experience this faith for yourself. G. K. Chesterton once said, "The Christian ideal has not been tried and found wanting. It has been found difficult; and left untried."

I believe you will find great benefit in reviewing your knowledge and experience of Christian faith. In what ways, if any, were you related to a Christian church during your first decade of life? What are your opinions of the Christian faith today? What Christians have you known personally who have been a turn-off to you? Are you willing to explore the faith firsthand? Have you had any type of encounter with Christ that seems significant to you?

Ponder these questions about the Christian faith for a day or two.

SEVENTH GUIDANCE: *Considering Jesus Christ*

*I saw the Spirit descending from heaven
like a dove, and it remained on him....
I myself have seen and have testified
that this is the Son of God.*

In the last Guidance I suggested that God is the name for your deepest hunger. Thus far I've referred to God as *the voice, mystery, other, another,* and *answer.* These words are pretty vague and need concreteness. Clearing up the vagueness is where Jesus enters our discussion.

I have emphasized to you the importance of a trustworthy tradition. In the framework of an established faith, our search for God will be helped by insights from the history of that faith, parameters set by the faith, the testimony of those who have lived the faith, and the guidance of wise and trustworthy persons.

Without telling the whole story, I want you to think of Jesus as a window through which you see God; he is the lens of your glasses. He is like an icon of God, one at whom you look while actually seeing through his transparency. The important thing is that he has God's very nature and shows us what God is like in human form. When we seek this concreteness, we turn to his deeds and teaching, including dying and rising from death.

Jesus reveals what we can know about God. The God who created the universe spoke through Jesus. God was joined to him in a way that means Jesus was truly a man and simultaneously God in our midst. If we wish to know God, we look at and listen to Jesus. He offers the key to the mystery of God.

I ask you to consider Jesus because of the sheer impact of his person on the world. Think about all the ways that his life and teachings have shaped our world. Time is marked by his birth. He has inspired colleges, universities, and hospitals. He has been the major subject of much of our art, literature, and music. The book that contains his teaching and the events of his life—The New Testament—has been the number one best-seller for centuries. Without depending upon religious confessions for our judgment, the amazing influence he has had upon world history makes him the most significant person who has ever lived. This towering person demands to be taken seriously by people of every generation.

As you begin to focus your attention on Jesus and attend to his words, I believe you will also begin to make several discoveries: the character of the one who breathed the breath of life into you, the clue of the voice that has spoken, the closeness of the other who has been with you on your journey, the object of your wondering as well as the guide to help you to God.

To illustrate this, let me tell you one of the stories about Jesus. It tells about his return to his headquarters along the sea of Galilee. Read it slowly and reflectively and ask yourself this question, "If God is like Jesus, what must God be like?" Use the words, actions, and attitudes of Jesus in this story, along with other people's reactions to him, to help you answer the question.

> When he returned to Capernaum after some days, it was reported that he was at home. So many gathered around that there was no longer room for them, not even in front of the door; and he was speaking the word to them. Then some people came, bringing to him a paralyzed man, carried by four of them. And when they could not bring him to Jesus because of the crowd, they removed the roof above him; and after having dug through it, they let down the mat on which the paralytic lay.

When Jesus saw their faith, he said to the paralytic, "Son, your sins are forgiven." Now some of the scribes were sitting there, questioning in their hearts, "Why does this fellow speak in this way? It is blasphemy! Who can forgive sins but God alone?" At once Jesus perceived in his spirit that they were discussing these questions among themselves; and he said to them, "Why do you raise such questions in your hearts? Which is easier, to say to the paralytic, 'Your sins are forgiven,' or to say, 'Stand up and take your mat and walk'? But so that you may know that the Son of Man has authority on earth to forgive sins"—he said to the paralytic—"I say to you, stand up, take your mat and go to your home."

And he stood up, and immediately took the mat and went out before all of them; so that they were all amazed and glorified God, saying, "We have never seen anything like this!" (Mark 2:1-12).

If God is like Jesus, what is God like? How does that match your image of God? This is a very important question to answer: What is your image of God?

EIGHTH GUIDANCE: *Observing his deeds*

They were all amazed
and glorified God, saying,
"We have never seen anything like this!"

One way to consider Jesus is to observe the things he did—his actions. The stories about him have been recorded in the New Testament portion of the Bible. The people who followed him carefully watched what he did, formed his miracles into short stories, and told them to friends. When Jesus' earliest followers gathered to worship God, they repeated his sayings and probably one or two of the stories about him. Eventually someone collected these various stories into a manuscript. The earliest collection of his sayings, miracles, and admonitions became the basis for the first three books in the New Testament—Matthew, Mark, and Luke.

Look at his acts recorded in the book of Mark: He cast out demons (1:23); he called disciples to follow him (1:16); he cured a leper (1:40); he calmed the fierce winds disturbing the sea (4:36); and he raised a little girl from death (5:35). Jesus did other miraculous feats like walking on the sea, calming the winds, telling his disciples where to drop their nets for a catch, and he multiplied loaves and fish to feed multitudes.

His disciples, with the intent of enlisting new followers, repeated these marvelous stories to demonstrate what Jesus could do with a human life. For example, they told about the leper who came to him requesting help. The leper said, "If you choose, you can make me clean" (Mark 1:40-41). Jesus responded immediately, "I do choose. Be made clean." As Jesus' followers told his story, their listeners identified with the leper and cried out, "If you want to you can make me whole." As his disciples told the story, the spirit of Christ filled the listeners' imagination and through the touch of Christ they were healed. These short, simple stories still have the power to transmit the presence of Jesus to us today.

Perhaps a brief witness will help you see what I mean. After twenty years of marriage, and ten of those twenty years spent in marriage counseling, my relationship to my wife got worse and divorce followed. I wondered if God could use a failure in helping others find faith. I had a strong sense of guidance to visit an Episcopal bishop. After listening to my struggle with God's call and my worthiness, he said, "I think you need a service of absolution."

He set the date, Wednesday before Thanksgiving. I met

him in the chapel. He went to the pulpit and began reading the story of the paralytic who was healed (Mark 2:1-12), the same story that I asked you to read in our last session.

In this story four friends of the paralytic brought the helpless man to Jesus. When Jesus saw him, he said, "Your sins are forgiven." A few religious snobs in the room wondered how a man like Jesus could forgive sin.

Then Jesus said words to them that I heard as if they had been directed to me. "Which is easier, to say to the paralytic, 'Your sins are forgiven,' or to say, 'Stand up and take your mat and walk'"? As the bishop read those words, it was as though Jesus sent me a telegram, "Which is easier, Ben, to forgive your sins or command you to get up and get on with your life?"

Then Jesus said to the paralytic, "Stand up, take your mat, and go to your home." And in those words he said to me, "Get up from your paralysis of failure and guilt, and get on with your life and work." And those words, from that day to this, settled my issue of whether God wants to use my life.

You can discover the power of the scripture to speak to you for yourself. Read the story of the leper in the first chapter of Mark (1:40-45), the second book in the New Testament. Picture in your mind the scenes: a leper approaches Jesus, he kneels, he cries out to Jesus, "If you want to, you can make me whole."

Jesus answers him, "Of course, I want to."

Imagine that you are the leper bringing to Jesus whatever keeps you from being close to God. He cares. He reaches out and touches you. Listen to his words to you.

What Jesus did in the days of his life on earth he continues to do through his Spirit! He speaks the same words, "Be made whole!"

Make this prayer like a mantra that you say silently through the day, "If you want to, you can make me whole!"

9 NINTH GUIDANCE: *Listening to His Words*

What an amazing discovery awaits you! The Christ who rose from death lives today and he still speaks. His speech most often flows through the words of the New Testament as it relates his miracles and his short sayings. It is as if he stands behind the words written on the pages speaking through those words to us today. I have told you about my experience of hearing him speak, and perhaps you now have your own story to tell.

During his life Jesus spoke about many things—birds, fish, cities on hills, seed and soils, parents, marriage, and children. But Jesus gave repeated emphasis to three or four things that lay at the heart of his message and ministry. Everything he said is important but he repeatedly emphasized three themes: the reign of God, the love of God and neighbor, and forgiveness. These baseline truths hold the same relevance for us today as they did for those who heard his words for the very first time. Think about these words, repeat them until they ring in your ears, and muse over them until they becomes his words to you.

The Kingdom of God

Jesus began his ministry preaching the "good news of the reign of God." He understood his mission as one that initiated a new age, a radical departure from power and personal glory that dominated other societies throughout the history of the world. By kingdom, Jesus meant an era when God's reign comes on earth. This new era will be a time of peace and well-being, an era of plenty for everyone. Jew and Gentile will become friends, and children, women, and slaves will become full participants in the new age. Under God's loving reign all wars will cease and peace will prevail. May the day soon come!

When Jesus spoke of the "reign of God," he thought of it as literally hanging over the heads of his hearers. This new order will bring peace, justice, and fulfillment to persons of all races, nationalities, and social locations without distinction. The reign of God presses hard upon the existing social order to transform it into an expression of God's loving will.

Love of God and neighbor

When a lawyer asked Jesus about the greatest commandment in the law of God, he responded with the requirement to love God and neighbor and oneself. A rightly ordered world begins with persons who have rightly ordered affections. To love God means that God takes priority in your life. To love God completely expresses itself in our doing the will of God. Our affections cannot be separated from our actions. In the Christian sense, love cannot remain in the will or the emotions but must express itself in love for neighbors, the people beside you.

Love means unconditional, positive regard for people in

your life and even those beyond the people you see and touch weekly. This loving attitude toward others means that we seek to find good in them, we think the best of their actions, and we value them as fellow human beings. And when these persons need our assistance we are there to help them.

On the personal level, loving our neighbor means responding to friends in need, to beggars on the street, and to those who suffer misfortune. At another level, loving the neighbor means helping victims of floods, storms, and catastrophes. In a larger sense, loving our neighbors involves political and economic justice. Being a disciple of Jesus ultimately signifies participation in a new world order.

Forgive others as you are forgiven

Jesus has always been big on forgiveness. All of us need forgiveness because we fail: We violate the rules of God's region; we fail to love in some hard situations and sometimes in easy ones too; and we hold grudges. These failures create a cancer in the soul and forgiveness opens the door for healing.

On one occasion a follower asked Jesus, "How many times must I forgive my brother or sister who sins against me? Seven times?"

Jesus answered, "I tell you seventy times seven."

This interchange has a deeper meaning than appears on the surface. When the disciple says "seven times," this implies complete forgiveness. Seven in the Jewish understanding implies perfection and suggests total forgiveness. Instead of affirming this "perfect" forgiveness, Jesus raised the requirement to the nth degree when he said, "I tell you seventy times seven." He called for perfection beyond perfection when it comes to forgiveness.

For one day, practice these teachings:

❧ Look for an expression of God's rule in our society (clue: find someone who visits hospitals and prisons or someone who is making efforts at world peace).

❧ Notice one expression of love demonstrated in a friend or a fellow-worker (when you get the courage, tell them you noticed their kindness).

❧ Intentionally forgive someone who offends you (like a rude driver on the expressway).

❧ Reflect on a day like this when you lived a forgiving life.

TENTH GUIDANCE: *Following Jesus*

Come follow me.

You have considered Jesus—his person, his words, and his deeds. I invite you to face the most important choice of your life, the decision to follow him! He walks into your life today, much as he did into the lives of those fishermen years ago. He speaks the same words, "Follow me." And he sets those who hear his call to the tasks he must accomplish in our generation. We today are on the front line of his initiative in the world.

How do you answer the call to follow him?

Let me clarify what this decision to follow him includes. First of all you follow Jesus as a mentor. As you know, a mentor is a mature person who has learned a great deal about life and how to live it. As your mentor, Jesus will show you how to recognize both your gifts and your opportunities to become the best person you can be and to serve God in the fullest manner. As his student, you will spend time getting to know him and absorbing his spirit. A mentor generally has a great deal of patience and encouragement in the process of helping someone learn about life.

To follow Jesus also means that you follow him as a student, a learner. When you begin reading the stories about Jesus, you will discover that his followers are called disciples, which means learners. Especially as you read Mark's account of Jesus' relationship with his disciples, you will discover that they have trouble interpreting Jesus' actions and they seem confused about his teachings. Yet, Jesus was exceedingly patient with them and repeatedly explained to them his message and mission. So when you become a student, Jesus will teach you about yourself and God's plan for history. He will teach you about how your destiny fits into God's plan.

One of the greatest deterrents to becoming a disciple arises from the fear that we do not know enough to follow him. Many are anxious about failing in their effort. A disciple, like every student, will certainly make mistakes and be forced to learn lessons a second or even a third time. There is no disgrace in failing, but not learning from our failures makes us look foolish. Jesus has amazing patience with slow learners.

You follow him also as an apprentice. In the trade language of a few centuries back, an apprentice attached him- or herself to a master to learn a skill. Generally, the commitment was to learn the skill of the master—stonemason, carpenter, painter. This apprentice relationship to Jesus has the same aim, to learn how to do what Jesus did. You know already that this has something to do with creating a relationship with God, healing the sick, liberating the poor, and seeking justice for the oppressed.

Do you see how following Jesus is a progressive appropriation of his will and his way? You choose to follow him. You look to him as a mentor who models what it means to be a Godly person. Like a mirror of your mentor, you pray that your life will reflect this loving God. You enroll in his school of discipleship to learn about the God he revealed and the kingdom he spoke of. And you attach yourself to him as an apprentice to learn the skill of living and loving God and the person next to you, your neighbor.

Speaking as one of his voices in the world today, I invite you to become a disciple of Jesus. This means that you make a decision to look to him as a mentor, you study him as a great teacher, and you attach yourself to the master as an apprentice. Sometimes this feels like a giant step and a scary one too. Let me make it simple for you.

Give as much of yourself as you can, to as much of Jesus' way as you understand, and do it now. Trust him to embrace you, guide you, and show you much more than I've said.

If you sincerely wish to make this choice, check "I do" on the line at the bottom of the page and sign your name.

( ) I do.

Your Name

11
ELEVENTH GUIDANCE: *Listening to the Voice*

Speak, Lord,
for your servant is listening.

The presence of the living Jesus means very little until we learn to listen to his voice and pay attention to what he is doing in our lives. Already you have heard of his promise to come back to his disciples on earth, to be with us, even to be within us. Still, a crucial question (about which many of us wonder) cuts right to the core—how do we engage this presence in our midst, in our consciousness? How do we communicate with him?

I believe that you and I can engage him in our consciousness by listening and looking, by opening our ears and eyes. But, you might say, if he does not act, how can we see? And if he does not speak, how can we hear? Be encouraged. He does act and he does speak. He wants to talk with you.

You cannot force a conversation with Christ, but you can position yourself to listen. Essentially we have two modes of consciousness: an active and a receptive mode. In your active mode of consciousness you ask questions, gather data, argue, deduce truth, and come to new insights and conclusions. In this mode you do your analytical, logical, inductive and deductive work. God has given you this capability to search for truth, and it is good.

But you also have a receptive mode of consciousness, and this is the best place from which to listen to God. In the receptive mode you let things happen, you do not make them happen. In other words, you are being acted upon rather than acting out. You are alert, open, and listening for ideas, images, and inspiration. In this mode you seek to notice what is happening in both your inner and outer worlds. In no way is this receptive mode intended to blank out your mind or lead you into passivity. Rather, it can be another avenue to truth.

Let me tell you about a young person who received a communication from the Lord. Not too long ago, a young lawyer came to talk with me about his decision to enter the professional ministry. I asked him to tell me what brought him to this consideration. In response he told me about a mission trip to Mexico and how he had encountered persons with deep faith and a peace that enamored him. We talked about that experience and the way it had influenced his life upon his return home. Then he paused and looked steadily at me for several minutes before saying, "I believe I can trust you with something that has been happening to me."

I nodded and waited. My friend Robert continued, "He's been talking to me."

"He has?" I inquired.

"Yes!"

"What has he been saying to you?" I asked.

"He keeps telling me that he loves me and he has something for me to do," Robert replied.

My new friend told me more about his interest in God, and about how wanted to find ways to serve God faithfully. But he had come to me to get my opinion about whether he should come to seminary and study for the ordained ministry.

But I said, "Robert, I believe God is at work in your life in special ways. What God is saying to you sounds very much like the God I know. Go on back home and serve him in your church and through your profession as a lawyer."

As he was leaving my office, I added "Keep listening to God."

He asked, "How can I do that better?

This is what I said to him: Set aside thirty minutes to listen to the presence inside you and around you. Find a quiet place, sit comfortably, and relax. Pay attention to your breathing; even count your breath in a monotonous way until you feel your body relaxing. Focus on the tension spots in your body and bid them dissolve and melt away. Keep at it until you are centered and quiet on the inside. In this receptive mode, think of an issue in which you need guidance. State it slowly. Stay focused. Let the ideas come to you. Notice the thoughts that emerge in your consciousness. After thirty minutes, write down the thoughts that came to you. Review these ideas. Which of them seem to speak to your situation? Note the ones that have a tone of conviction to them. Live with them for a few days to see if they persist. If they stay with you in a convincing manner, make a simple response of obedience to the word that has been spoken to you.

Perhaps what I said to Robert will help you begin to deepen your own practice of listening to what God is saying to you.

12
TWELFTH GUIDANCE: *Using Old Words in New Ways*

Let your word be "'Yes, Yes"
or "No, No'"
anything more than this
comes from the evil one.

You may discover some "yes, yes" words and some "no, no" words that work with your common, ordinary speech.

For a day's experiment I invite you to use words that you've spoken dozens of times before but with a different meaning. Perhaps you've said them at a movie, or at home, or at work. These are the words of your common speech: "Wow!" "Thanks." "Pardon me." "Help me." "Help them."

First, I want to help you use these words in relation to God whom you are meeting through Jesus. Begin with Wow! "Yes, Yes" to God.

"Wow" often expresses an overwhelming feeling when we experience beauty, massiveness, or mystery. "Wow" is the kind of word that wonder evokes. When you stand before a majestic mountain and it makes its mark upon you, you utter "Wow!" When you think of the greatness of God, the mystery of the cross, and the divine interest in us humans, "Wow" is all there is to say. Say it now: "Wow!" In the long history of God's people this expression has been called praise. Praise is the human response to this great God when we see the marvels of creation, encounter the mystery of simply being, or experience God's goodness, forgiveness, and mercy.

"Thanks." A word to say for things you appreciate.

You've said this to a friend who opened the door for you or bought your lunch. The word is as common as getting out of the bed. Think about your life, your relationships, the world you live in, and the people who love you. Does the thought of these blessing also evoke a word of thanks? Feel your gratitude. Say "thanks" out loud. In the Christian tradition, thanksgiving has always been a main track.

"Pardon me." Anyone with a smidgen of etiquette has said these words when stepping on someone's toe or walking through the door ahead of another or bumping a fellow passenger in the elevator. These two words contain a kind of magic that creates and sustains relationships. This simple expression, "Pardon me," fits neatly into our relationship with God and those with whom we live and work every day. Not one of us acts perfectly, so we always need to be pardoned by those valued persons in our lives. Can you not recall people you have hurt? Or can you think of times that you have failed others? When you have hurt God by your thoughts and actions, there is forgiveness for the asking.

"Help me." I know you've asked for help at some point in your life. Maybe it was before you took a test or in preparation for a job review or when you felt in danger, you called out or whispered under your breath, "Oh, God, help me." In the Christian tradition this prayer is called petition, asking help for yourself.

"Help me, her, or them." In our everyday life we've asked individuals to help persons in need and they have responded. The request may have been to help the beggar on the street, a fellow-worker in the office, or an older child to assist a brother or sister with homework. We also use these words in times of illness, pain, or crisis to request God's aid for our friends, acquaintances, or family members. In a time of crisis you often hear a newscaster state that our prayers are with the victims. The Christian tradition calls these requests intercessory prayer, asking God's help for others.

These common, street-type words take on a whole new meaning when they're uttered as prayer. When we address them to God, these ordinary words become a new and different kind of language. They become prayers.

I suggest that you use these five expressions in two ways. First, take five minutes before you get out of bed and say "Wow!" in response to the mystery and beauty of a new day to live before God. Say "thanks" for one thing in your life, "pardon me" for a failure. Then think of something that you want for the day and ask for it. Ask God to help someone you know who needs God's assistance. Repeat these same words when you go to bed tonight. Second, at some point during the day, pause and fine something you can say the five words about. Listen to the words again: "wow," "thank you," "pardon me," "help me," and "help them."

THIRTEENTH GUIDANCE: *Learning a New Language*

His disciples said to Jesus,
"Lord, teach us to pray,
as John taught his disciples."

You have begun to use common words to speak with God. Other words, words tested over a long period of time, offer us help in the practice of prayer.

After the first disciples of Jesus had followed him for a time, they asked him to teach them to pray. They had observed Jesus at prayer. Probably they connected his all-embracing love and his spiritual power with these times of communion with God. They yearned to participate in the same reality they had seen manifested in him.

In response to his disciples' request for help with their prayer, Jesus offered them a model prayer. He offered them a way of prayer that touches everything essential to our life with God and our life in the world. Here is a brief explanation of the prayer he taught them.

"Our Father." God is not my father only, but yours and all persons. Father means one who loves and protects us like a good father. In an age of paternal abuse, the word *father* has been corrupted for some. If this has been true for you, try other words like *mother, lover, helper,* or *rock.* The Bible uses different words to refer to God. If *father* gets a positive response from you, feel free to use it.

"Who is in heaven." God dwells over all persons, as well as being in us and with us. This phrase makes it clear that we are not God but we are subject to God, as are all persons.

"Hallowed is your name" means we reverence God's person. This name means God's character, presence, power, and being. We don't cheapen it with crass expressions or casual references, but rather we save the name "God" for a very special person, the one who created and loves us.

"Your kingdom come on earth as it is in heaven" expresses the desire that peace, justice, compassion, freedom, and all good things come to the human family through God's gracious love. *Kingdom* refers to the reign of God that Jesus taught about. Our prayer requests God's rule or reign over all things.

"Your will be done on earth as it is in heaven" almost restates the previous petition Jesus taught his disciples to pray. God's will for goodness and love takes shape in God's kingdom and so we pray that all persons may do God's will.

Notice how all these requests focus upon God—God's name, God's kingdom, and God's will. The next three petitions relate to our needs—food, forgiveness, and guidance.

"Give us today the bread we need." Note the plural. The request is not "give me" but give all of us in the human family the basic needs required for life. Bread symbolizes all the necessities for life.

"Forgive us our sins as we forgive those who have sinned against us." We not only need food for the body but forgiveness for the soul. Forgiveness repairs the breach between God and us and offers freedom from failure and shame. God hears and forgives. You will notice some churches pray forgiveness for our trespasses, as well as the debts and sins of others.

"Lead us not into temptation but deliver us from evil" is a petition seeking God's guidance written in a way characteristic of Hebrew poetry. On the one hand, we ask God to do one thing but not to do another. Lead us—not into temptation but deliver us from evil. This request focuses on our need for God's wisdom that leads us into the meaning and fulfillment of our lives.

The prayer of Jesus, as normally prayed in church, concludes with a burst of praise and adoration: "For yours in the kingdom and the power and the glory forever and forever. Amen." If you knew no other prayer, this one prayer of Jesus would suffice for all your needs.

I have four suggestions for you in the use of this prayer. First, I encourage you to begin memorizing it, if you have not previously committed it to memory. Second, when you have memorized the prayer, try to say it all the way through without letting your mind wander, even one time. Each time your mind wanders, begin praying the prayer again.

Third, think deeply about each phrase, like "Our Father who art in heaven." Hold these two words (*father* and *heaven*) in your mind and notice the feelings and ideas they attract. Proceed with each of the major phrases. "Your kingdom come," etc. Do not rush through the prayer. If you come to the end of your quiet moments and have not finished thinking and praying this prayer, pick up the next time where you left off.

Fourth, say this prayer with the gathered community of Christ in a church. As you pray it with the Christian family, recall how you stand in a long tradition of worshipers who from the time of Christ have prayed this prayer.

FOURTEENTH GUIDANCE: *Meeting God by Praying Your Life*

> *Jesus himself came near*
> *and went with them ,*
> *but their eyes were kept from recognizing him .*

When religious people think about coming face-to-face with God, they often recall the time when Moses went up to the mountaintop to receive the commandments of God. While he was meeting with God, the mountain quaked amid the flashing of lightning and the roar of thunder. In other examples of meeting God, we picture the prophet Isaiah in the temple seeing visions and confessing his unworthiness to be in the presence of the Holy God. Or Christians often think of the voice that spoke from heaven at Jesus' baptism. Or we recall how tongues of fire, a fierce wind, and speaking in tongues accompanied the coming of the Holy Spirit upon the disciples of Jesus in the upper room.

I do not doubt that the Holy Spirit comes into the lives of persons in extraordinary ways. I believe the unusual events surrounding the giving of the law to Moses, the speech from heaven at the baptism of Jesus, and the coming of the Spirit after the ascension of Jesus, are the honest efforts of trustworthy people to describe meeting God. In contrast with those demonstrations of the holy presence, however, I would like you to think about meeting God in the ordinary events of an average day of your life. Meeting God in the happenings of your life offers hope and encouragement for people like you and me who likely will not hear a voice from heaven speak to us. When we begin to expect God to meet us, we discover quite quickly that God is not far away but is here mixed with the common, everyday experiences that shape our lives and give substance to our choices.

If God is not in our waking and rising, in our going to work and returning home, in the quiet spaces and in the numerous contacts of the day, then our encounters with the Holy Spirit are limited to special times and special places. A God who only inhabits special times and places seems rather remote from the lives of ordinary folk. I'd like you to turn this special-time and special-place notion on its proverbial head and affirm God's presence in every place at all times.

Once you make that shift, your perspective changes from wondering when and if God will come before you, to *where* and *how* God is coming into your life. A ride to work becomes an adventure of seeing God in other drivers or sitting next to one of God's messengers on the bus or plane. When you are looking, perhaps you notice the kindness of God in a person with whom you work. In unexpected events that normally would cause stress, you feel a calmness and certitude, and you begin to suspect that another has been in that moment with you.

Would you like to discover that the great love of God is actually in your everyday life? To do so, you might begin this day with the expectation that you will meet God sometime during the day. Try to be sensitive to God's coming and going in your drive to work or your morning break or during a telephone call or an encounter with a friend or fellow employee. Perhaps it will be a neighbor, a fellow student, or someone on the train or bus. Be expecting.

At noon, review the morning to see if there's any sign that God spoke to you and touched your life in some unexpected way.

In the evening, gather up the day, think of the different engagements of the day as short paragraphs in your life story and wonder about the meaning of these short episodes. At least, give thanks to God for your life, for the happenings and opportunities of the day, and for the people you have met. Wonder what message God may have sent you through the events of this day.

When I review yesterday, I see a portion of the day spent writing this very material. I went to work at noon. At 1:30 P.M. I had an appointment with a Chinese pastor, a former student in the school where I taught, who had been driven out of Indonesia after his church was burned and his life threatened. I listened to his tragic story and sympathized with his need for a job. Immediately I thought of two persons to call on for help. One of these persons suggested another name to contact. Last night I passed a church with a Chinese congregation meeting in its building, and I wondered if they needed ministerial help. When I asked the pastor of the church where I was leading a discussion, he offered to make contact with the neighboring pastor to see if they had a place for my friend.

When I reflect on these events, six hours in duration, I wonder where God was in my former student's coming for help. Did God put the names of persons in my mind to telephone? Was it an accident that I noticed the church with a Chinese service? Somehow I believe God was at work in the simple events of this otherwise ordinary day.

15

FIFTEENTH GUIDANCE: *Writing a Dialogue with Jesus*

A lawyer, asked [Jesus] a question to test him.
"Teacher, which commandment
in the law is the greatest?"
[Jesus] said to him,
"You shall love the Lord your God
with all your heart,
and with all your soul,
and with all your mind."

During his earthly life all kinds of persons entered into conversation with Jesus. Both religious and political leaders and women and men in desperate straits asked him questions, sought his wisdom, and requested his help. He never ignored any of them and generally responded positively to their entreaties.

Take, for example, the lawyer who asked Jesus which was the greatest commandment in the law. Jesus could have ignored his question or interpreted his question as an attack, but he did neither. Jesus took the question at face value and answered in a straightforward way.

I have discovered that writing a dialogue with Jesus about the deepest issues in my life opens the door to a warm, intimate relationship with him. In communicating with Jesus, I feel that I am able to draw upon a transcendent wisdom. Because this has had such importance in my life, I want to introduce you to a way of listening for the voice of Christ in your heart.

To prepare you for writing a dialogue with Jesus, read from the Gospel of John, chapter twenty-one, verses four through seventeen (John 21:4-17). This story focuses on Peter's coming ashore when he recognizes the risen Jesus Christ standing before him. Jesus serves his doubting followers breakfast and engages Peter in conversation.

As you enter into the environment of that beach breakfast, imagine that your fishing companions, after breakfast, get in the boat, take the fish, and begin paddling up the lake to Capernaum. You are now left alone with Jesus sitting on a huge rock beside the sea. Picture that scene in your mind. You have an opportunity to converse with Jesus Christ about anything you wish.

The process of writing a dialogue with the living Jesus is quite simple. Get pen and paper and find a quiet place. Get seated comfortably. Take a few deep breaths and become still on the inside. Keep centering yourself until you are quiet deep within. Become fully receptive to the presence of Christ.

When you have made proper preparation, ask Jesus the question that most naturally and easily comes to you. Pause. Listen to the words that come into your consciousness and begin writing. Don't edit the words that come to you, simply write them on the paper before you.

Let these thoughts flow out of your consciousness right onto the page before you. Write until your thoughts cease.

Read what you have written. Open your mind and heart for a response. Again let your response flow naturally out of your depths. I urge you not to edit your thoughts, judge neither what you write nor what you hear. Let the conversation take place between you and Jesus without inhibition.

Continue this dialogue back and forth until you have nothing else to write and the flow of words has stopped coming into your consciousness. Aim for at least six interchanges with Jesus in this dialogical fashion.

As you look over your writing, wonder if there was something more than your own wisdom speaking the words and forming the thoughts that you wrote in the dialogue. In a sense, all these words came from you, but as you read them, do you begin to wonder if someone else might have been inspiring your thoughts? I encourage you to keep a soft attitude toward what you have written. Don't claim that Jesus gave you every word. Dismiss neither the flow of thoughts and words as nothing more than your own imagination.

I recall having the urge to write a tract on "The Language of God." As I thought about the notion, it seemed to me that it was quite presumptuous for me to think that I could take on such a task. So I asked Jesus the question, "Isn't it presumptuous of me to think that I could write about the language you speak to human beings?"

Quick came the reply in my consciousness, "Not if I told you to, it isn't!"

So one day I will write that tract.

16 SIXTEENTH GUIDANCE: *Exploring the Book*

All scripture is inspired by God
and is useful for teaching,
for reproof,
for correction,
and for training in righteousness.

If you have made the journey through these spiritual exercises to this place, you have come a fair distance. You've demonstrated a strong interest and intention to know the God who is revealed in Jesus. You have begun to embrace some of the practices he taught his disciples. Indeed, you are well on the way toward discovering the meaning of being a disciple of Jesus Christ.

As you progress on this journey, it is crucial for you to become acquainted with the source book of the Christian faith. I am referring, of course, to the Bible. As you respond to my guidance in this session, it will help if you have a Bible before you as I introduce its contents.

Recently I participated in a conference that attracted numerous young adults who had little acquaintance with the Bible. A pastor, sensitive to the situation, led one of the teaching sessions. In the first session he asked members of the class to pick up their Bibles and open it at the middle. He then instructed class members to turn to the left until they came to the second book in the Old Testament, Exodus. While pages were turning, he suggested that older members of the class follow the same procedure so that persons who did not know the order of the books would not feel conspicuous. With this experience informing my own approach, please do not think that I am being too basic or simplistic as I introduce you to the content of this religious library.

Pick up your Bible and turn to the table of contents and note the two major sections. Place your finger at the beginning of the New Testament. Hold the book up and look at it. What do you notice as you open the book with your finger?

The Old Testament contains the scriptures of the Jewish faith, but they are also foundational scripture for the Christian faith. Christianity has its roots in the faith of the Jewish people but goes beyond Judaism. For Christians, the New Testament describes how Jesus, a Jew, revealed God in a special way, and his revelation became the cornerstone of the new Christian faith. The New Testament also shows how Jesus made things right between God and all persons through his death and resurrection.

Now turn back to the Table of Contents. Read aloud the names of each of the books in the Old Testament. Think of the Old Testament and the New Testament as a library that contains a number of books. The first five books are known as the Pentateuch—"the five books"—or the books of Moses. Joshua through Esther relate the history of Israel written from the perspective of their relationship with God—their struggles, their failures, their defeats, and their triumphs are catalogued with great honesty.

The book of Psalms, and then Job, Proverbs, Ecclesiastes, and the Song of Solomon constitute worship-and-wisdom literature. The book of Psalms, for example, was the prayer book of Israel. From the earliest days, Christians also have prayed these psalms, offering their worship to God. You will find a psalm for every human experience and emotion.

The books from Isaiah to Malachi relate the messages

God sent to Israel through specially chosen persons called prophets. Prophets were normally ordinary people who participated in the religious life of Israel. Under some strange circumstance God was often shown to the prophets and called them quite often to speak hard messages to Israel, such as calling the nation to turn from its evil ways and do God's will. In different periods of Israel's history, from Samuel through Malachi, various prophets arose to speak to concrete, historical situations in the life of Israel.

In the New Testament, you will find four types of literature: the Gospels, the Acts of the Apostles (a stylized history of the early church), and the letters of the apostles to churches, to individual people, and to specific groups of Christians. The last book in the New Testament, Revelation, provides a symbolic picture of the end of the world and the triumph of the love of God over all the forces that have resisted it. In the book of Genesis you find the beginning of the story of God and human beings and in Revelation you read the ending.

Now for a little closer look at the New Testament: The first three books of the New Testament, Matthew, Mark, and Luke, describe the life of Jesus from three different perspectives. The fourth gospel, that of John, has the character of a meditation on the life of Jesus inspired by his Spirit. The Acts of the Apostles describes the beginning of the church and how it functioned during its first century. The letters of Paul, Peter, James, John, and Jude are responses to specific needs in the churches of the first century.

The Bible is like a library containing sixty-six books. Thirty-nine are in the Old Testament and twenty-seven are in the New Testament. You will find it the source book of your faith because it tells about God's revelation to the world, first through a covenant with Abraham, then the pronouncement of law through Moses, and finally the coming of Jesus Christ.

For your assignment, begin memorizing the books of the Bible in the order of their appearance. I think it will help you to remember them in sections. In the Old Testament remember Pentateuch (the first five books of Moses), the books of history, wisdom, literature, and the prophets. Remember the New Testament sections: the Gospels, Acts, Letters, and the Revelation. This assignment will help you immensely in finding your way around the Bible.

SEVENTEENTH GUIDANCE: *Hearing God Speak*

Today
this scripture has been fulfilled
in your hearing.

I have shown you how the "living" Jesus speaks through the Holy Spirit in our intuition and imagination. He also speaks to us through the words recorded in the Bible, our sacred scriptures. I want to show you several ways in which he speaks to us through scripture. In this guidance I will focus on one of the most basic ways. Very simply, Jesus speaks to us by our asking questions about a particular selection from the Bible.

When I was seventeen years old I read the Bible for the first time. Prior to that time in my life I may have read a verse in Sunday school or in a church program, but I had never personally examined the Bible to find out what it said. For me the world and language of the Bible was a strange, new world. Believe it or not, I could actually read these scriptures and make some sense of them in my life. The simple approach that I want to show you would have been of enormous help to me the first time I tried to read this text for myself.

Open your Bible (if you don't have one yet, purchase a New Revised Standard Version of the Bible). Turn to the New Testament and look at the second book, Mark. Read chapter three verses one through seven (Mark 3:1-7). This selection of scripture relates the story of Jesus going into the synagogue, a Jewish place of worship, and seeing a man worshiping there whose hand was deformed.

A little background information about this setting may be of help to you. The Sabbath day was a day of rest for the Jews because God rested from creation on the seventh day. The Herodians constituted a political party supporting King Herod. The Pharisees belonged to a strict religious group that was meticulous in keeping the laws given through Moses. (Refer to the second book of the Old Testament, Exodus, and read chapter 20 for an account of God's giving the law to Israel.)

With this modest background, I invite you to read Mark 3:1-7 slowly, thoughtfully. Ask yourself these questions:

1. What is this incident about? What subject does it explore?

2. When this story was later told to Jesus' followers, what did they hear? What did they understand the story to mean?

3. When you read this passage of scripture, what relevance does it have for your life? How does it connect with you? (Incidentally, one of the amazing things about Jewish and Christian scripture is that

the words, images, and thoughts actually speak to us in our present situation.)

4. What will you do with the insight you have been given? How will you incorporate it into your life?

When I ask these questions of the story of healing the deformed hand on the Sabbath, I have thoughts like these:

1. The healing of the man with a deformed hand focuses attention on Jesus' willingness to break one of the laws of Moses (as it had been interpreted by the Pharisees) in order to help a suffering person. It is about compassion and reinterpreting the law.

2. When the early church heard this story, they may have thought of Jesus' power to heal them. Or, they may have taken hands to symbolize work for God, and Jesus' power to make our hands work well enables them to work properly for God's purposes.

3. In this story I hear Christ speaking to me about healing my hands so they may be engaged in his work today. The hands that I use to write books also need to become hands that feed the hungry.

4. I will begin to look for ways to serve those persons less fortunate than I.

These questions will help you squeeze meaning for your life today out of other incidents in the ministry of Jesus. Furthermore, this way of questioning particular passages of scripture provides a method for studying all scripture.

Why not try it on your own by reading Mark 1:40-45?

18

EIGHTEENTH GUIDANCE: *Stopping! Looking! Listening!*

[Jesus] stood up to read,
and the scroll of the prophet Isaiah
was given to him.
He unrolled the scroll
and found the place where it was written:
"The Spirit of the Lord is upon me..."

Jesus himself read and knew the scriptures of the Old Testament. As a child he had attended the synagogue and participated each year in the great festivals in Jerusalem. Just as it was critical for Jesus' mission that he knew the scriptures, it is likewise important for the followers of Jesus to read and understand the Bible. We are fortunate to have the record of what he said and did as remembered by his earliest followers and written for our benefit. These writings give us the primary teachings of Jesus and they report his amazing deeds. The first four books of the New Testament tell us about Jesus' life and ministry and the Acts of the Apostles, the fifth book in the New Testament, describes how the "living Jesus" worked in and through the small group that believed in him.

My last guidance invited you to work with a passage of scripture for yourself. In reading about the healing of a leper, you may have felt awkward trying to connect with a man who lived hundreds of years ago and who was suffering an incurable illness. People often feel inadequate for the task of reading and interpreting scripture. It is as if they think they might do irreparable harm to the text. Fear not. The New Testament can withstand your assault. Read, then stop, look, and listen to what it is saying to you.

You will benefit greatly from reading large portions of scripture at one time. For example, try reading the story of Jesus in one sitting. I recall a particular Sunday afternoon when I first had this experience. Shortly after Jesus had become a personal reality to me, I read the entire Gospel of Mark in one sitting. Mark's account of Jesus' life covers about three years. You can read it in two to three hours and gain a sense of his life from the beginning of his ministry until his crucifixion, burial, and resurrection from the dead.

After getting an overview of Jesus' life, read the Gospel of Mark more slowly, reflecting on it as you read. Then divide a sheet of paper into two large columns. Above the left column write, "What Jesus Did." Above the right column write, "Teachings and Questions." In the left-hand column note each significant act Jesus performed as recorded in Mark's account of his life and ministry. Your entry could include preaching, the calling of followers, the performing of miracles, etc. Toward the end of Mark you will notice how Jesus prepares the disciples for his death and the testing of faith they will face before the Resurrection.

On the right side of the sheet, note the substance of Jesus' teachings and your questions. On this second reading of the Gospel of Mark, you might note his parables of the soils, the treasure, or the pearl of great price. You may have a question about Jesus' statement that whoever does the will of God is his mother and brother. What does he mean by this statement? Write your question. After reading a few chapters, you may find it important to ponder your questions and perhaps discuss them with someone who has additional insight into scripture.

For your personal benefit, when you hit upon a word or

phrase that really speaks to you, that seems to rise off the page and grasp your attention as if it were meant just for you—stop, look, listen. When you come to the verses that have affected you most strongly, underline them with a red pencil. After a few days, review the underlined verses. Note the kinds of insights you receive from your reading.

If you are wondering why I stress the importance of reading the story of Jesus, the answer is simple. Christian faith is centered in the person of Jesus. To be a disciple, to become aware of Christ's presence and to hear him, requires you to know about his life and teachings. You will be engaged in this school of discipleship all your life, and I am trying to give you a simple but enduring approach to learning the ways of Christ.

I am confident Jesus Christ will speak to you as you read the Gospel of Mark and note his deeds and teaching, along with your questions.

NINETEENTH GUIDANCE: *Entering into the Story*

[Two disciples of John]
came and saw where [Jesus] was staying,
and they remained with him that day.

After reading the story of Jesus' life and ministry as told to us by Mark, did you ever think how marvelous it would have been if you had been there when Jesus healed the blind man or fed the five thousand?

One of my favorite places on the Sea of Galilee is called the Primacy of Peter. This is the spot where the church has chosen to remember the resurrection of Jesus. Peter and the other disciples of Jesus had given up hope. He and several of his friends had returned to Capernaum and begun fishing. In the early morning, while they were searching for fish, he and his companions noticed Jesus on the shore with a fire already made.

Peter was so excited he jumped into the water and waded to shore, not waiting for his companions in the boat. Jesus prepared breakfast for them and then had a most interesting conversation with Peter. What must these followers of Jesus have felt as they sat on the beach with him, eating the food he had prepared, knowing all the while they had given up hope? Yet he responded to them as friends and served them freely.

On numerous occasions I have sat where tradition says this incident took place. I have looked at the lake and then the statue of Peter with a shepherd's crook, pondering what it must have been like on that morning when Jesus appeared to these followers who had given up hope. Sometimes it has seemed like I was there with them. The stories of Jesus provide us with the material for an encounter like this with him.

Being there, being present to a text of scripture, opens us more deeply to Christ. I have introduced you to several ways of understanding a particular selection of scripture. In this exercise I would like to help you discover another way that the "living" Jesus can speak deeply and personally to you through an account of him meeting his disciples on the beach. Open your Bible to the Gospel of John and read chapter twenty-one, verses four through seventeen (John 21:4-17).

Permit me to show you how to be present in this scene. In achieving this sense of participation, I will invite you to use all your senses in an imaginative way to be present to the risen Christ, to Peter, and to his companions.

In this encounter between the risen Christ and his followers, hold for reflection several aspects of the story: discouraged disciples in their boat, not having caught any fish; Jesus on the shore, a fire burning, conversations among the disciples, and the conversation between Peter and Jesus.

1. Close your eyes and imagine you are Peter in the boat. Feel the boat rocking. Look down at the dark water and think how it compares with the darkness in you. Look at the sky. It is early morning; sunlight is beginning to break. See the mist rising from the sea. As you pull in the nets, feel the cords cut into your fingers. Inhale deeply and feel the cool, damp air in your nostrils and then sense it filling your lungs. How do you feel about having fished all night and caught nothing?

2. Suddenly you hear a voice that seems faintly familiar. "Friends, have you caught any fish?" You answer, "No, none." The voice tells you to cast the net on the opposite side of the boat. You cast and the net fills with fish. What do you feel when you obey this simple direction? What emotions do you experience when the voice addresses you as "friend?"

3. Suddenly you feel that you know this voice that has called out to you. You are shocked, frightened, and eager to see the speaker's face. Think about these feelings. Let yourself engage this experience with Christ more deeply.

4. Envision yourself walking over the rocks at the water's edge and casting yourself down before Christ. If you are Peter and you have denied that you know Jesus, what do you feel in his presence? You gave up hope and went back to your old profession.

What does that mean now as you stand in Christ's presence?

5. Picture yourself and the other disciples eating breakfast with Christ. What does this remind you of? What are you thinking as you sit on a large rock eating fish and bread with Jesus and your friends?

6. As you have identified with the character of Peter, write a firsthand account of your experience of this sequence of events. You might begin, "After he died I was so discouraged that I went back to fishing, and..." Take your time. Adopt a receptive attitude. Begin to write and let the words flow through you. Don't edit the thoughts that come to you. Keep writing as long as any words come to you.

Read over what you have written about Peter's encounter with Jesus on the beach. What do you discover about yourself in what you wrote? What do you discover about Jesus? What happened in Peter's relationship with Jesus?

Pause to reflect on the thoughts that have bubbled up in your mind as you have participated in this ancient story and wonder how God may be speaking to you today.

20 TWENTIETH GUIDANCE: *Practicing the Text*

> *Not everyone who says to me,*
> *"Lord, Lord,"*
> *will enter the kingdom of heaven,*
> *but only the one*
> *who does the will of my Father in heaven.*

Perhaps you wonder why I am spending so much time guiding you in reading and experiencing Christ through the scriptures? But nothing informs and inspires faith like hearing the spirit of God speaking to you. Although God speaks in many ways to us, all these words must be judged by the teaching of the sacred scriptures. The truth of these scriptures springs from a long, rich, and dependable tradition, and without it we would be cast upon the restless sea of chance without compass or map.

My guidance for you in this lesson consists of the Christian art of phrasing, paraphrasing, and practicing the scriptures. Each of these movements draws us closer to God, making us agents of a better world.

Phrasing. I am using this word to indicate the practice of repeating verses of scripture as a way of forming our lives. For example, each morning when you get up you might quote a short verse of scripture in your mind. "This is the day that the Lord has made, I will rejoice and be glad in it" (Ps. 118:24). This simple practice would be a great way to begin every day with a positive, wholesome, and expectant outlook.

If you are anxious about your future, you might during the day quote, "So do not worry about tomorrow, for tomorrow will bring worries of its own. Today's trouble is enough for today" (Matt. 6:34). What a wonderful reminder to keep our trust in God.

Paraphrasing. Still another way to uncover the truth of our lives is through paraphrasing the Bible. By paraphrase, I mean read a few words from the Bible, think about the meaning of those words, and then rewrite them in your own words. Amazing transformations come through the practice of transposing the words of scripture into your own words. For one thing, you begin to understand the text. You cannot transpose words of scripture into your own words until you know what the words meant in their original setting.

Once you understand the words in their context, you begin to search for words in your vocabulary that communicate those same meanings. Do not forget that your vocabulary has been conditioned by your experience. As a consequence, each of the words you choose has a variety of connections to your life that are invisible to others and possibly to you also. So as you paraphrase the words of scripture, your choice of words connects the scriptures ever more deeply within your own experience.

Another change occurs through paraphrasing. The first level of your paraphrase lies close to the original words, but as you continue to rewrite these words, they draw more and more of you into the text. Do you see how the first paraphrase of a text serves like a magnet to draw other words, colored by different experiences, into connection with the text of scripture? Slowly but surely rephrasing scripture fuses your life with the text.

Practicing. I am using the word *practice* much like it is used by professionals in particular fields of service. A doctor practices medicine, a lawyer practices law, and a teacher practices teaching. All of these professionals use their knowledge to do the work of their calling. Christians practice the truth of the scriptures, or at least they aim to. In one sense, phrasing and paraphrasing aim at changing the way you live your life. The text of scripture has not done its work until it effects concrete changes in us.

To help you engage in this threefold movement with the text, I have chosen one of the famous sayings of Jesus, "You shall love the Lord your God with all your heart, and with all your soul, and with all your mind" (Matt. 22:37). Try phrasing this verse each day when you arise. Let it be a reminder of your most important goal, the all-inclusive goal of your life.

Let me illustrate how to paraphrase this teaching of Jesus. "I, Ben Johnson, am to love God above everything else. To love in this manner means that God is to be first in my life. Loving God like this is not a mere nod of the head. I am to love this God in a manner that does not demean any person. If I love like this, I cannot judge and criticize others. When I tear others down, I not only cause pain for God but I sow the seeds of destruction in my own life." I choose to love God by showing kindness to all God's creatures, to be patient with those who test my love and with those who do not reciprocate it.

For your learning, I invite you to work with Matthew 6:19-21. These verses refer to our values, the things we treasure most. Choose a few words to "phrase" during the day. Read these words, grasp the ideas intended, mull them over, and then paraphrase them at several levels of your experience. As you read your paraphrase think of the ways it touches specific parts of your life and how it sheds new light on who you are and what your life is about.

Before you paraphrase this text, you might ask yourself questions like these: What are earthly treasures? What are heavenly treasures? What is the difference? How do you store up either or both?

21

TWENTY-FIRST GUIDANCE: *Digesting the Text*

How sweet are your words to my taste,
sweeter than honey to my mouth!

If you seek to live in accordance with the teaching of the scriptures, one of the greatest struggles you face is getting the truth of the text into your life. This issue constantly presses down like a weight continually upon our shoulders. How do we get the truth of the text not only into our minds but also into our hearts? Truth in the mind builds knowledge, but a knowledgeable head standing alone is like a tank full of gas with no spark in the motor to ignite it. Truth in the heart ignites the fire, creates heat, and explodes into energy, driving us to act.

To illustrate how the truth of the text migrates from the page of the Bible to the mind of the reader and then to the heart, think of eating a grape. First, you take the grape in your hands and examine it. Next you touch it to your lips and let it fall into your mouth. Once the grape passes your lips, you begin to chew it, crushing the skin. After you swallow the pulp, your digestive system changes it, and distributes it throughout your body. The grape now becomes part of you as you metabolically ingest the grape.

In a similar way, the truth of a text becomes part of you when you read it prayerfully, think about it critically, and ingest it into your soul. Read it. Get it in your mind. Ask questions about it. Ask God to join the truth of the text to your life so that you think, feel, and choose in ways harmonious with the text. Amazing change begins to occur as you feed upon the word of scripture.

Exercises in digesting the word of God yield amazing discoveries. Read the saying of Jesus, "Blessed are the peacemakers for they will be called children of God." Read it until you can say it to yourself without looking at Matthew 5:9. Say each word slowly and pause. Blessed...are...the...etc., until you have ended the verse. As you say each word let it stand before your mind's eye until you have fully examined it.

When you have memorized the words of Matthew 5:9 begin to expand each of the words or phrases until it touches your life. *Blessed.* What does the blessing of God mean? How would I be made happy in making peace? How would I affect others? When you have finished with *blessed,* move to the next phrase—*are the peacemakers*—and think what these persons are like. Where do you need to be at peace? With whom do you need to be at peace? What are the disruptive things in your heart today? Keep saying the text, *Blessed are the peacemakers....* Let this text lead you more deeply into the presence of Christ and the peace that he has to give you and that he wills to offer others through you. Continue pressing the words and thoughts until you have an idea of what it means at this point in your life for you to set about making peace.

Most likely this one tiny saying of Jesus will make you aware of your own needs. When thoughts of your needs or those of others come to your mind, pray for peace. Your deep thoughts about peace and peacemaking will make you aware of how much you need God's help to become a peacemaker.

When you have finished biting, chewing, and

swallowing this peacemaker text, let it descend into the depths of your mind and rest there. From this central point of feeling and choosing, the truths that have touched your mind will become part of your being, your way of living.

Remember: *Blessed are the peacemakers for they are children of God.*

22
TWENTY-SECOND GUIDANCE: *Waiting before the Word*

**For God so loved the world
that he gave his only Son,
so that everyone who believes in him
may not perish
but may have eternal life.
Indeed,
God did not send the Son into the world
to condemn the world,
but in order that the world might be saved
through him.**

You can actually feel the magnetism of the Word drawing you to God. The work of the word of scripture does not serve itself, it brings us to God. In some ways, the text is like a magnet that attracts your hunger and draws you through its truth into God. In another sense, scripture is like a copper wire that transmits the energy of the Spirit into your heart. These two movements should not be looked upon as contradictory but complementary. And yet, to shift metaphors, scripture provides a window through which to look at God.

Whether serving as a magnet, conductor, or window, the

key is that scripture provides contact between the divine Spirit and our human spirit. This dynamic encounter between the holy and the human often occurs when we look at the text, through the text, and finally beyond the text. Each of these sensory metaphors provides a movement—a movement from God to our self and from our self to God. Scripture aims to bring us into an intimate relationship with God.

Probably no verse of scripture is better known or more easily recognized than the one I cited at the beginning of this guidance, John 3:16. Let the truth of this affirmation of Jesus sink into your consciousness. God so loved the world. The Creator takes delight in the creation, cares for it, protects it, and willingly forgives human failures. You, as a creature of God, are loved and loved unconditionally. Dare you permit yourself to feel the depths of this love?

Because God loves us, God gave his son. God permitted Jesus to live and suffer as a human being. God even permitted him to be crucified to show us how much love God has for us. God loves human beings enough to suffer and even to die for them. Jesus' dying on the cross rips open God's heart to show us the extent of divine love for each of us.

Everyone who believes…may have eternal life. This statement opens the door for us—you, me, everyone—to enter into a relationship with this God of love now and forever. The real presence of God chooses to come into history in a genuinely human life, to demonstrate what it means to live on earth. Each of us by trusting in Christ can participate in this eternal life.

Look at this text. Read it. Ask questions. Does this text not draw you toward God? Does it not give you energy for living? Can you see through Jesus Christ and beyond him to the kind of God with whom you are dealing?

You will discover that another text (John 3:17) offers the same rich gifts. I will not direct you through it, but I do want you to focus on one truth if offers: God did not send the Son to condemn you but to save you. If, like so many, you live with self-condemnation, negative judgment of yourself, or self-rejection, give it up. Christ came to free you from these negative perceptions of yourself. Let God love you!

Spend whatever time you need to engage fully these truths within your mind, within your emotions, and within your imagination. But keep clearly in focus the fact that you are being energized by God and attracted by God who has come among us in Jesus Christ.

When you meet God at the center of your being, a gentle breath calms your spirit. In the peace of God's presence, go out to live your day. But throughout the day, return to your center to feel the peace that was established when you were touched by the presence of a loving God. And remember often, *God did not send the Son to condemn the world.*

23

TWENTY-THIRD GUIDANCE: *Considering Jesus Again*

> *Consider him*
> *who endured such hostility*
> *against himself from sinners,*
> *so that you may not grow weary*
> *or lose heart.*

I invite you again to consider Jesus, the son of God. Earlier we looked at his person, his teaching, and his deeds in order to decide whether or not to follow him.

Now look at Jesus as a model for your life. As you read Mark's Gospel, you discover how Jesus' earthly life ended. After three years of ministry, one of Jesus' disciples betrayed him and turned him over to the authorities. Another of his followers denied any association with Jesus. All the others left him when the final test came.

The Jewish religious leaders took Jesus into custody, examined him, and turned him over to the Roman rulers in Palestine about 30 A.D. The representatives of Rome conducted a trial, condemned this good man as a common criminal, beat him, mocked him, stripped off his clothes, and nailed his hands and feet to a cross and killed him as he hung between two thieves. As his body hung between heaven and earth, he prayed, Father, forgive them for they do not know what they're doing (Luke 23:24).

This amazing act of forgiveness, this prayer for forgiveness puts teeth in Jesus' words, "If you forgive others their trespasses, your heavenly Father will also forgive you; but if you do not forgive others, neither will you Father forgive you your trespasses" (Matt. 6:14-15). Jesus' words make clear the necessity of a forgiving spirit.

Two kinds of forgiveness will open you more fully to the forgiveness of God. First, clearing up old resentments, hurts, and broken relationships will open the way for a joyous, forgiven life. From whom do you need forgiveness? Name the oversight, slight, injury, or betrayal. Accept responsibility for whatever may have been your part in the painful incident and ask the other for pardon. If you feel too shy to speak to an individual face-to-face, write a note requesting forgiveness.

Asking forgiveness is never easy. I can usually find a dozen reasons not to apologize or even admit that I have been wrong. Recently I went to the pharmacy for a prescription. The pharmacist has never been particularly friendly. I asked him to fill the prescription for me. He made a remark about why he couldn't fill it at the moment. I responded harshly, feeling rage in my stomach. His reply carried the same tone as my confrontational words. Finally he gave me the medicine and I left.

I did not pray well that evening or the next morning. The face of the pharmacist kept coming into my mind. Finally, there was nothing left for me to do but apologize to him for my rude behavior.

I went by the pharmacy, got his attention, and said, "I was rude to you yesterday and I want to apologize. There is no excuse for my behavior."

He said, "That's okay."

The issue was settled. My only cost was a tiny piece of ego. I still have plenty left.

Now the second type of forgiveness: not only must you be forgiven, you need to forgive. Forgiveness is a two-way street. Be forgiven and forgive! Today practice the gentle art of forgiving others their offenses. Consider forgiving those who cut in front of you on the freeway. Forgive those who make negative statements about you. Forgive those who ignore you, blame you, or speak harshly to you. Forgive and forget. If you fail or find it difficult, turn to God in serious prayer and ask for forgiveness and the strength to keep on forgiving others.

My wife often says that I never forget the failures of others. Maybe she says that because I don't buy tires from a certain manufacturer who would not replace defective tires. I don't trade with a restaurant that charged me for a baked potato I did not receive. And I don't use a particular charge card because of the company's lack of concern for customers. In no form have any of these businesses asked for forgiveness.

But there was a friend of mine who had made some

terrible mistakes. I had tried to help him but he would not listen. In the last days before he moved from our city, I had very strained relations with him. After about two years he asked me to address a group of church people in his area. At his insistence I agreed.

He picked me up at the airport and on the way to the speaking engagement he brought up our recent past. He said, "Johnson, I know that you have been unhappy with some of my choices the last few years. Perhaps I was wrong, but whether or not I was wrong, I don't want to sacrifice our friendship."

"You don't have to," I said. "I also don't want anything in me or in our past differences to separate us."

The wall came down. The relationship was repaired with a little forgiveness on both sides. To be a follower of Jesus means that we live with an open, forgiving attitude.

Also remember to be kind to yourself, even as God is kind to you. Forgive yourself when you fail!

24 TWENTY-FOURTH GUIDANCE: *Showing Compassion*

"If you choose, you can make me clean."
"I do choose. Be made clean!"

One indelible image of Jesus that burns in our memory is the compassion he showed to others. All kinds of people sought him out desiring his healing love. A blind man cried out to him for help. Lepers approached him. A woman with persistent bleeding and the father of a dying child both came to him for help. Jesus responded to each of these persons seeking his compassion.

In a world of vicious competition, ruled by the notion that we all must take care of ourselves, virtually no place has been made for gentleness, kindness, and helpfulness. As a consequence, people get crushed as the wheels of commerce roll over them or as they are beaten down by the strong and thoughtless. The followers of Christ are sent forth each day to bring healing and hope to those who suffer broken spirits and alienation.

Acts of compassion, little deeds of love, need not be a dramatic rescue or a bold announcement of self-sacrifice. Simple acts of caring from the heart will plant compassion just as yeast when mixed with flour causes it to rise and change.

Three metaphors may help you be more compassionate throughout the day: a caring heart, a listening ear, and a helping hand. When you see pain in another person, search your heart and let it matter to you. When someone approaches you with a problem or concern, give a listening ear. And when you see a fellow human being in need today, reach out with a helping hand. With deeds like these you can make the world a better place.

When I think of having a caring heart I think about Bonita. Her friend Richard was dying of cancer. Every week she called his wife, Mary Ann, to ask how Richard was getting along and how she was holding up. She didn't talk very long because she knew about the pressure of living when death stared you in the face. Yet her short phone call supported Mary Ann through the ordeal. Mary Ann said it made all the difference to her. You probably know many people like Bonita.

You also may have known a man like Burney. He had the kind of listening ear that not only heard what you said but also heard what you meant. I've never known anyone who heard the words behind the words like Burney. His listening ear and his wisdom changed my life. No, it saved my life. When I spoke at his memorial service, I began with the statement, "Burney saved my life; anything else I say is mere commentary on that fact." After the service, a dozen people said to me, "Why didn't you ask us to raise our hands because he had saved our lives too?"

I have in my mind the perfect image of the "helping hand." Willie C. was a plain man but a good man. I doubt he finished high school, but he possessed a doctorate in being available when a friend needed him. His friend John was elderly and unable to cut the grass around his house. So every week Willie C. came to John's and cut his grass, took out his trash, and helped fix up the screen door. John died after ninety-two years. When the will was read, John left Willie C. one percent of his estate. I am sure Willie C. was the most surprised man in the room. A helping hand costs so little and it's never offered in hope of a reward.

Today as you go forth in the world, a bearer of the light of Christ like a city set on a hill, let your love flow out to all of those around you. May I invite you this day to be deliberate and intentional in looking with your eyes, feeling with your heart, and touching with your hand to make a difference in this world?

25

TWENTY-FIFTH GUIDANCE: *Giving Yourself Away*

*It is more blessed to give
than to receive.*

You have been seeking to learn the way of Christ by
permitting his spirit to express forgiveness and compassion
through you. I wonder how it feels to be developing a
Christ-style life? How would you answer the question if a
friend asked you today?

As you continue reading about him, you've doubtless
been struck by the absence of greed in Jesus. What you
see in Jesus epitomizes self-giving—his time, his attention,
and his life.

Not only did he live a sacrificial life, Jesus urged his
followers to give themselves away. He said, "Give to
everyone who asks of you and do not refuse anyone who
wishes to borrow from you" (Matt. 5:42). Think of the
beggar on the street holding a homeless and hungry sign,
or the one standing at the traffic light who seeks to wipe
your windshield for a dollar. Instead of being repulsed or
judging the person as a deadbeat getting money for booze,
give what you will. But before you give your money, ask
the recipient one question: "Tell me, if you will, what
brought you to this point in your life?" Give your new
friend the benefit of the doubt, let your beneficiary have
all the time required to answer your question. Perhaps
your listening ear is a greater gift than your open hand
with money in it.

Jesus also said, "Give, and it will be given to you; good

measure, pressed down, shaken together, running over, will be put into your lap. For the measure you give will be the measure you get back" (Luke 6:38). I dare say the act of giving will reward you sufficiently. It will turn your focus from yourself to others. It will crack the greedy, grasping spirit. Your generosity will give birth to love. What a return on your investment!

While I was in graduate school and short of funds, I met a man from Korea who was in greater need than I was. I shall never forget giving my last $20 to a person who did not ask for help but gave every evidence of needing it. An unbelievable thing happened to me that very day. Before six hours had passed, a friend of mine took me out to see a new subdivision he was developing. While we were talking, he asked, "Would you mind if I gave you a $100 to help with your needs?" An amazing return on a twenty dollar investment!

Let me tell you another story. My former mentor told me about Danny and his marvelous inspiration. He urged me to visit Danny in one of the great Florida cities. While making plans was not easy, I finally fit the trip into my schedule. I attended worship in the church where Danny was the minister. The experience of worship was good but not great. What was great was the vision Danny had for helping people give themselves away. He really believed that we humans cannot outgive God. He challenged persons to give time and money. His way of issuing the challenge fascinated me.

Over lunch that Sunday Danny described the challenge he had issued to the congregation. He had challenged each one to a thirty-day experiment that included attending worship, giving two hours of service through the church, arising at 4:00 A.M. to give attention to God in prayer, and giving ten percent of his or her income for one month. All these were serious challenges for those who participated in the experiment, but the fifth challenge spoke loudest to me.

Danny challenged all the members of his congregation to "do one, kind, unselfish deed each day without hope of reward." What a challenge! What a way to empty kindness and compassion into a hurting world!

I want to challenge you with this fifth discipline. Each day for one month intentionally do one kind, unselfish deed for someone in your life. Don't do it for reward of any kind. Show your love because you love!

Each day, at the end of the day, reflect on what giving to others has meant to them, and what it has meant to you.

26 TWENTY-SIXTH GUIDANCE: *Witnessing to the Truth*

You will be my witnesses
in Jerusalem, in all Judea and Samaria,
and to the ends of the earth.

Have you yet become amazed at how the Christian faith, which began in a small country three thousand miles from you more than nineteen hundred years ago, has now made you part of its grand procession? How did Christianity survive the Jewish denial and the Roman persecution and become a worldwide faith?

The answer to this intriguing question is actually very simple. People like you, very ordinary people like you and me, who had met Jesus became his ambassadors. These enthusiastic followers went into every corridor of their social world with the spirit of Jesus and his message. As they told their stories of forgiveness, love, and personal transformation, Christ spoke through their lips to eager listeners. When those who heard the original witness told others, the same amazing changes took place in them also. So from one person to another, from one generation to the next, the Christian faith in the power of personal witness has passed from the first century to the twenty-first century. How amazing and thrilling that Christ uses every one of us to help others know him.

Your witness for Christ flows from at least four aspects of your life. You communicate Christ to others by simply being a follower. Others will notice a new kind of energy flowing from your life. They will feel his presence through you like heat radiating from a stove. Some will sense a spirit of love and generosity in your manner of life. It requires almost no risk to express Christ in your life.

Actions are important also. What you do will be noticed by others and will become an unconscious witness on your part. When you practice compassion for people with whom you work, others will see it. If you take time to help a street person, passersby will see your concern. If you have been impatient with members of your family, they will feel a new patience through your more relaxed style. Remember, you never do these Christian deeds to be noticed but because you seek to follow him. Doing these things for show will be bad for you, and it won't help others either.

Some of the best witnesses I know are listeners. At first glance, thinking of a listener as a witness may seem strange, even contradictory, but it is true. In a noisy world in which most people are vying for air time, listeners are growing scarcer. As you learn to listen perceptively, ask a few well-chosen questions, respond gently, and you will become an effective witness. Someone has said that "we must learn to listen to one another through to the point of discovery and disclosure." Permit others to talk long enough to discover who they are and disclose it to you, a sympathetic listener.

In addition to being, doing, and listening, witnesses also tell their story—not the whole story but small vignettes of Christ's work in their lives. At this point in your voyage of faith, you have accumulated enough experience to begin sharing your discoveries or struggles that reflect your efforts to follow Jesus. As my direction to you today, I invite you to join this long line of witnesses reaching back in time some twenty centuries.

Ask Christ to show you the one person to whom you may tell part of your unfinished story. If this endeavor feels a bit scary, consider these factors: Christ will be with you and speak through you. Isn't that pretty amazing? There are persons you can communicate with today better than at any other time in your life because at another time you will be in a different place. You are today the best Christ-person someone knows. When you ask Christ to show you the person to speak with, expect him to do it.

I recall, as though it was yesterday, my very first experience of sharing a bit of my faith with another person. Fred Lee and I were working at the Bus Station Café in my hometown. I was a brand new follower of Jesus and full of joy and excitement about this new adventure. No one had instructed me to let others know about Jesus in my life. I was so full of my newfound faith that it spontaneously flowed out of me. When I approached Fred, he said that he did not know anything about Jesus but would like to. He permitted me to tell him what I knew of Jesus. What a gift to me! Fred too began to follow my new friend, Jesus.

By the way, you don't have to have all the answers, nor

do you have to have all your problems solved. Simply be open to telling what you currently know about this new way of life of following Jesus Christ. No one needs a snooty, self-righteous, pushy witness. Others desire from you compassionate love and a gentle story.

27

TWENTY-SEVENTH GUIDANCE: *Seeking a Companion*

*Do two walk together unless
they have made an appointment?*

An old African proverb says, "So that one can blow dust from the other's eye is the reason that two antelope walk together." This ancient wisdom expresses a profound truth about our life in the spirit of Christ. This new life that has been given to us requires relationships; it lives through connections with others. We need each other to save us from self-deception and self-centeredness. We also need relationships with others to overcome our sense of loneliness and the despair of an isolated life. Each one of us needs the other to blow the dust from our eyes.

Our baptism into Christ, being joined to him and possessing his spirit, makes companionship possible. This sacred act of the church has already joined each of us to every other person who is joined to Christ. As you continue your journey in faith, be aware that all others who love and follow him have similar needs for companionship. They too may feel lonely, estranged, and separated from the deeper meanings of their lives; the answer often comes through a connection with others.

I urge you to begin searching for someone with whom

you may share this journey. In the early days of my following the way of Christ, I knew little about a formal, agreed-upon relationship of spiritual friendship. My help came from caring people in the community of faith. One of those in my church was a dentist who took me under his care. He asked me to meet with him each evening when he closed the office. Day after day he instructed me in the faith, shared his wisdom with me, and prayed for me. I cannot remember anything in my early days of faith that had such a profound effect upon me. Someone may reach out to you and invite you into a supportive, nurturing relationship. But if not, I think you will benefit from taking initiative in searching for a person to be a companion for you.

When you choose a companion, make a few basic decisions about the relationship. Meet weekly if possible, and at least once each month, to talk about exciting discoveries you are making in your life with God. Agree to talk with each other about your experiences of praying, reading scripture, and caring for others. Pray for each other out loud before you end your time together. Finally, set a time for the next meeting.

A good challenge for you to work on with your companion is to use this book. Begin at the First Guidance and share with your companion what has taken place. If you cover one guidance at each meeting, it will take about six or seven months to cover the guidance given in each of these directives. I don't believe it would be dull because, after all, I have spent a lifetime learning the insights that I've shared with you.

Here's another really challenging idea: When you tell the story of your newfound faith to others, give him or her a copy of *A Seeker's Guide* and offer to meet with that person weekly to share what you have learned. In the most basic way imaginable, you will pass your faith on to another and will learn from that person by reviewing these exercises and giving more attention to each one.

Don't be afraid of your ignorance. You already know more than you think you know and you know more than those who have not begun walking in the way of Christ.

Invite a companion to be like the antelope. Walk together and blow dust out of each other's eyes.

28 TWENTY-EIGHTH GUIDANCE: *Making Peace*

*Blessed are the peacemakers
for they will be called children of God.*

In a world that is growing more hostile and violent, Jesus' mission of peace holds renewed hope. It promises a calmer, gentler, safer world. At the time of his birth, angels sang, "On earth peace to those whom he favors." Whenever his name is mentioned these words ring in our ears—peace, peace, peace!

Today, Jesus urges us to be at peace with ourselves. Lay down your spear and shield! Stop the vicious civil war inside between your true self and some imposter who has taken up residence. Fantasized greatness can never be a match for the truth of your created self.

Be at peace with your neighbor, the person next to you. Lay down your guns of judgment and your missiles of condemnation. The shiver of fear and the sharp jabs of jealousy disrupt your peace, and if unleashed they will destroy the subject of your raging imaginations. Be at peace with your world! Your God made it good, but the freedom that came wrapped in goodness has unleashed world-destroying powers. Call on your nation to stop the killing! Tell your leaders that they cannot make peace by declaring war. Retribution is sure: Those who take up the sword will perish by the sword.

Blessed are the peacemakers for they shall be called the children of God. When you make peace with yourself, with your neighbor, and through your government with the nations of the world, you will show that you are a child of the God of peace.

Do you have any idea what it feels like to bridge the chasm that separates you from another person? Have you ever been on the receiving end of a person seeking to make peace?

One experience of peacemaking that stands out in my mind still challenges me. A doctor whom I had known for a dozen years called to make an appointment. On the day he arrived at my office, I had no idea why he had come. He sat down at the table and began the conversation like this, "I have come to ask your forgiveness." I was a bit startled by his confession but I listened.

"I have been angry at you for the last six years. You were a spiritual leader and you got a divorce. I was deeply disappointed in you and I resented you for failing Christ and me."

At this point, I could have tried to explain. I could have shared with him that I too felt disappointment with myself. Or I could have told him the truth about how difficult life had been for me for twenty years. I did none of these things. I simply listened to him as he continued.

"I want you to forgive me for my judgment of you and for the resentment I have harbored. I'm getting to be an old man and I want to clean up the dark places in my life."

"Ed," I said, "I do from my heart forgive you. I hope also that you will forgive me for failing you and God."

Peace was made. It was sealed with a prayer, a handclasp, and a hug.

You too can be a peacemaker. It's never too early to begin.

During this week, act on three measures of peacemaking. First, identify that one thing for which you regularly condemn yourself. Resolve for one week to cease beating up on yourself.

Second, search the pages of your memory to discover the one person toward whom you feel the most anger or the person that you have misjudged or mistreated. Graciously forgive yourself and intentionally forgive that person and be at peace. If you have the courage, report your peacemaking activity to him or her.

Finally, send an E-mail letter to your senator or congressperson and describe your desire for peace in whatever situation our nation is threatening war.

Do these things and the God of peace will be with you.

TWENTY-NINTH GUIDANCE: *Assembling Together*

And let us consider how to provoke one another
to love and good deeds,
not neglecting to meet together...
but encouraging one another.

You may think it strange that I would seek to guide you in *how* to go to church, rather than *why* go to church. I can name a number of whys: you have been baptized or determined to be; you are part of Christ's body; you need the affirmation and support of others; you have gifts to offer that are hard to identify and use apart from the community of faith. To sum it up, you are not a Christian Lone Ranger. For all these good reasons, we should gather together with God's people. But instead of giving reasons as to why you should go to church, I am interested today in guiding you in how to gather with God's people.

When you go to church, try to forgive some of our members for falsely representing Jesus in their aberrant behavior. You can worship God much better if you don't get hung up on all our failures. None of us is perfect, but some of us could better represent Jesus.

Go to church to worship God, to acknowledge God's absolute worth, goodness, and beauty. Remember worship is first for God's sake and not for ours. These suggestions may help you before you get to the building. Once you are seated in a sacred place for the worship of God, you will find an order that includes being called before God, offering God praise, thanksgiving, and a confession of wrongdoing. It will also include places to listen for God to speak in scripture and sermon. You will hear prayers for members, the nation, and needy situations around the world. Examine the movement of worship a bit more closely.

Worship generally begins with a word or a song that invites us to come into God's presence, to recognize that we are before God. This is often designated "a call to worship." When that invitation is issued, in your heart pray, "I am here to offer my worship to you, O God."

Generally, the group gathered (a group we call a congregation) sings words of thanks or praise to God from a hymnal (a book of songs and readings). The words of the hymn constitute a prayer, so as you sing along or follow the words, make them a prayer in your heart.

After this hymn of praise, the minister will lead in a prayer of confession and the whole congregation joins with the minister to confess their corporate sins. We always ask for God's forgiveness because we have sinned in thought, word, and deed during the week. Join in by acknowledging that you share responsibility for some of those sins also.

After the prayer of confession, the minister speaks words of assurance that you are indeed forgiven. Listen to the minister's words as though Christ himself spoke them. Often the minister says, "In the name of Jesus Christ, you are forgiven." Believe it. Live in the confidence this week that you are freely forgiven for all your sins and failures.

The choir will sing an anthem (a special song). The music and words are intended to express to God the congregation's affirmation and praise. Follow the words sung by the choir and the feelings stirred by the music.

A leader of worship reads words from the Bible. Listen to the reading as God's words to the whole congregation and to you. When the minister preaches, try to listen as if God were speaking directly to you and the whole congregation through his or her voice. Listening to the sermon as God's word to you will change your attitude and your response.

At some time during the worship, an offering will be made. Whether you give one dollar or one hundred dollars, think of the dollar as a symbol of your whole self. As the plates are taken forward and the prayer of dedication is offered, think of yourself as being represented in that plate by the gift you've made and let your whole life be dedicated anew to God by this act.

All churches celebrate the grace of God by breaking and eating bread and drinking wine. Christians call this meal

Eucharist or Holy Communion. Sharing in this sacrament, as we refer to it, is a way of remembering Christ and receiving him into our lives. When you recognize Christ as your lord, you will want to participate. The service of worship closes with a benediction (blessing). The minister offers the blessing that you may go forth to forgive, make peace, and be a witness for Christ. He/she assures you that Christ is with you, surrounding you, and guiding you.

Live your faith throughout the week and return to worship next Sunday.

THIRTIETH GUIDANCE: *Praying for the World*

*Indeed, God did not send the Son into the world
to condemn the world,
but in order that the world
might be saved through him.*

Never get the impression that prayer reaches no further than your family or your own needs. One caricature of prayer goes like this, "God bless me and my wife Bess, our son and his wife Tess, us four and no more. Amen." Prayer cannot be domesticated like this self-centered couplet.

God cares for the whole world, all of God's good creation. God did not send Jesus into the world to judge and condemn it but to bring it back to God and to God's ways. If this is God's will, all the followers of Christ should daily be about the task of praying for the world that God's kingdom may come and God's will be done on earth as it is in heaven.

When Jesus came into Galilee after his baptism, he did not come to the people to judge and condemn them. Rather he came to invite them into a new way of life. During his sojourn in Galilee, Jesus met persons in distress—lepers, the demon possessed, or the blind and deaf—and he did not discount them because of their maladies. At moments when the disciples tried his patience by missing his intent, he forgave them and persisted in teaching them God's ways. The church has always seen the cross of Jesus as God's answer to a broken, alienated, and destructive world.

In your imagination see yourself standing beneath the cross of Jesus. He, a good man, has been judged, condemned, and is now nailed to a wooden cross to suffer a common criminal's death. Those responsible for his death taunted him, gave him vinegar to drink, wagged their heads at him, and mocked him for saying he was God's son. He prayed for those very persons who were killing him, excusing them because they were ignorant of their sin. He suffered in the burning sun for six hours. He surrendered his spirit to God. They ripped open his side with a spear and water and blood gushed out.

The suffering, pain, and death of Jesus Christ embodies God's message to the world. "I love you this much," God says. "I love you enough to identify with you, suffer for you, and die so that you may have life." This compassion calls us to pray for the whole world.

I have a special way for you to pray, a way for you to participate in God's concern for the whole world. Think of the newspaper as your prayer reminder, and as you read the news, translate the stories and reports in the paper as a call to prayer.

For example, when you read the headlines, ask yourself where God may be in the event reported. Do you give thanks to God or do you ask God's help for persons or a nation? Or do you ask for the forgiveness of both?

When you read articles that describe pain, loss, and suffering, pause a minute asking God's help for the persons you do not know and the circumstances you cannot fully understand.

As you scan the local news, you will find issues in which leaders need God's guidance and help. Ask God to give it to them. Surround the decisions of your leaders with prayer.

When you read the sports page, pray for us who make idols of teams and praise them for winning. When we place sports above the worship of God, our devotion to the game has gotten out of control. Pray for us.

The Travel & Leisure and the Homes & Gardens sections of the newspaper might lead to gratitude for beauty, for the beauty of creation and the renewing of the earth.

The Obituaries invite us to pray for all who mourn their losses, even people whom we do not know. The newspaper can serve daily as your call to prayer for your community and for the whole world. It can lead you out of yourself into a compassionate perspective on the whole world.

THIRTY-FIRST GUIDANCE: *Remembering*

I will call to mind
the deeds of the Lord;
I will remember
your wonders of old.

You have probably discovered already the weak spot in any faith—forgetfulness. This is a constant temptation for each of us who practices faith. The aging are often plagued with memory loss, but on the Christian journey forgetfulness is not confined to the aging—it affects us all. No matter how close we may get to God, no matter how often we see God's hand in our lives, we tend to forget. Is it because our minds become dull or do we forget because we get trapped in our daily rituals? I really don't know why I so easily forget my insights and good intentions, but I do. We forget who we are, what we are about, and why we chose this way of life.

In the book of Psalms, the prayer book of Jesus and Christians, repeatedly we find expressions like, "I will call to mind," and "I will remember." The people who spoke these words, like us, tended to forget. By recalling the deeds of the Lord or some special mercy they had experienced, they reoriented their lives and rekindled the fire of their devotion to God.

Note this prayer in Psalm 42,

These things I remember, as I pour out my soul:
how I went with the throng,
   and led them in procession to
   the house of God,

with glad shouts and songs of thanksgiving,
　　a multitude keeping festival.
Why are you cast down, O my soul,
　　and why are you disquieted within me?
Hope in God; for I shall again praise him,
　　my help and my God.

My soul is cast down within me;
　　therefore I remember you
from the land of Jordan and of Hermon,
　　from Mount Mizar (vss. 4-6).

Notice how the psalmist prays when he is depressed and thinking that the presence of God is far away. He remembers going with great crowds to the Temple to worship God. He remembers singing songs of thanksgiving and praise. He remembers the festive spirit. Then he wonders why his soul is cast down or depressed.

Our psalmist then remembers how God helped the nation cross the Jordan River and take the land before the mountains of Hermon and Mount Mizar. Recalling these feats of the Most High gives encouragement and strength to his soul. This psalmist was well rehearsed in the practice of remembering.

In the art of following Christ, we do well to practice the discipline of "remembering." I think some matters call for a rehearsal more than others. For example, remember your first hunger for God. Recall how God first met you. Consider once again how you experienced God's kindness when you failed again and again in a particular area of weakness. Revisit the greatest miracle of your life. Remember God's goodness and mercy to you.

What happens to you in the experience of remembering is really quite amazing. Around all of your sacred experiences swirls the power and energy generated in the divine-human encounter, and it is waiting to be tapped.

When you recall those moments of divine encounter, you absorb the empowerment associated with those experiences. So in these sacred venues resides a kind of reality that enables you to go forward with your life. The grace of God inhabits all your memories of the sacred.

As my final suggestion to you, I invite you to return to the First Guidance. Review it and the others that follow. Review in your memory the experience it first created in your mind, then in your experience, then in your heart. If you strike one of those directives that left you blank, you might try it once again to see if it will now yield its truth to you.

Finally, thank you for letting me be your companion and guide on this journey.

Your friend,
Ben Johnson

Warmly, wisely, gently, Ben Johnson leads the reader through the basics of Christian faith. Not a doctrinal primer, not an ethics text, *A Seeker's Guide to Christian Faith* is instead an introduction to ~~what~~ Christians have agreed upon for millennia. This ~~book~~ guides readers in self-examination, alerts ~~readers~~ presence in their lives (which they may have overlooked), and helps readers understand the language of faith. Along the way, Ben Johnson uncovers ways of praying, of finding God in worship, scripture, and acts of charity. Through thirty-one brief "Guidances," the author offers tools for spiritual growth that the reader may use at his or her individual pace.

Spiritual pilgrims, anyone who has ever wondered about the mysteries of life, searchers considering the Christian community perhaps for the first time—all will find here understanding and help.

A leader's guide is also available with this book for those wishing to use it in group sessions or in spiritual direction. You may also download the *Leader's Guide* at our website: **www.upperroom.org.**

BEN CAMPBELL JOHNSON,
the author of over 35 books, programs, and pamphlets, is the Professor of Christian Spirituality at Columbia Theological Seminary in Decatur, Georgia. Prior to that, he was director of the Institute of Church Renewal, a nonprofit, charitable foundation.

UPPER ROOM BOOKS™

ISBN 0-8358-0907-2

9 780835 809078   90000